Developmental Screening in Early Childhood: A Guide

5th Edition

Samuel J. Meisels and Sally Atkins-Burnett

National Association for the Education of Young Children
Washington, DC

Developmental Screening in Early Childhood: A Guide. 5th ed.

National Association for the Education of Young Children
1509 Sixteenth Street, NW
Washington, DC 20036-1426
202-232-8777 or 800-424-2460
www.naeyc.org

Through its publications program the National Association for the Education of Young Children (NAEYC) provides a forum for discussion of major issues and ideas in the early childhood field, with the hope of provoking thought and promoting professional growth. The views expressed or implied in this book are not necessarily those of the Association.

Carol Copple, *publications director*; Bry Pollack, *senior editor*; Malini Dominey, *text design and production*; Sandi Collins, *cover design*; Ingrid Patrick, *copyeditor*; Leah Pike, *editorial assistant*

Library of Congress Control Number: 2005930700
ISBN-13: 978-1-928896-25-8
ISBN-10: 1-928896-25-1
NAEYC Item #121

About the Authors

Samuel J. Meisels is president of Erikson Institute, a graduate school in child development located in Chicago. One of the nation's leading authorities on the assessment of young children, he has published more than 150 articles, books, and monographs and is a coauthor of the *Work Sampling System*, the *Early Screening Inventory.Revised*, and *The Handbook of Early Childhood Intervention*.

His research focuses on the development of alternative assessment strategies for young children, the impact of standardized tests, and developmental screening in early childhood. Recently, he completed work on the development of *The Ounce Scale*, an observational assessment for children ages 0–3 and their families, and is conducting a new study of its validity funded by the Head Start Bureau.

Dr. Meisels joined Erikson in January 2002 after 21 years at the University of Michigan, where he is now professor emeritus. Before becoming a faculty member at Michigan, he served at Tufts University as professor in the Department of Child Study and director of the Eliot-Pearson Children's School. A former preschool, kindergarten, and first grade teacher, he holds a doctorate from the Harvard Graduate School of Education.

Sally Atkins-Burnett is an assistant professor of early childhood special education at the University of Toledo. She teaches courses in early childhood education and special education. Dr. Atkins-Burnett has worked on the development of assessments for several national longitudinal studies including the *Early Childhood Longitudinal Study–Kindergarten Class of 1998–1999* (ECLS-K). She served as an expert consultant to the *Early Childhood Longitudinal Study–Birth Cohort* and the *Pre-Elementary Education Longitudinal Study*. She has published articles and chapters related to assessment in early childhood education and special education, and holds a doctorate from the University of Michigan. She has taught preschool, elementary school, and special education in public and private schools and has provided early intervention and consultative support to families and programs that serve children with disabilities.

Contents

Preface

*t*his guide was first published as a monograph on developmental screening by the Massachusetts Department of Education in 1978. Since then it has been rewritten and revised four times by NAEYC. Its intended audience is broad, including early childhood teachers, trainers, and administrators; policy makers; and those teaching in community colleges and undergraduate and graduate programs.

Each time this guide has been revised it has been possible to update it and add new information. This edition contains revisions of the text throughout, new reviews of screening instruments, and an entirely new annotated bibliography. For the first time, it also includes sections on screening for social and emotional concerns and screening individual areas of development. It is only because the field of preschool screening continues to evolve and remains important for children, families, and communities that it is possible to update this book.

Screening is not an end in itself. At its best it is a first step toward preventing a child's developmental problems from becoming more exaggerated, or a way of confirming that problems of learning and development are probably not present in a particular child. Anyone who asks children and families to participate in screening and then does not use the screening data as it is intended is wasting resources and possibly wasting human potential by not helping needy children become eligible for intervention at the earliest possible opportunity. Further, anyone who uses screening instruments with weak reliability or validity or who uses instruments for a purpose other than the purpose for which they were devised is likely to obtain inaccurate and misleading information. Such uses should be avoided at all costs.

As this guide makes clear, screening is a relatively simple procedure. It can be very effective and has the potential for improving the lives of children and families when appropriate instruments and methods are used. We hope this document will facilitate that process.

What Early Childhood Educators Should Know about Testing

*t*esting continues to expand its reach and broaden its impact on America's schools. The *No Child Left Behind Act of 2001* has been responsible for a virtual explosion of testing in public schools. Although the law as originally written only required testing of children beginning in third grade, more testing of younger children is taking place than ever before—much of this as a result of federal mandates. For example, 2003 was the first year that the Head Start National Reporting System was administered. That twice-yearly achievement test now is given to more than four hundred thousand 4-year-olds every year. Despite serious questions about the validity of the test raised by practitioners, researchers, and even the General Accountability Office, children's scores on the test may eventually be used to decide which Head Start programs will continue to receive funding and which will be closed.

Such achievement tests are very different from the tests described in this guide, in which we are discussing developmental screening instruments. Unlike achievement tests, which measure knowledge or skills a child has learned, developmental screening tests identify at an early point which children may have learning problems or disabilities that could keep them from realizing their potential. Developmental screening tests provide initial information for teachers that can facilitate individual children's learning, rather

1

than motivating teachers to teach to the test. Developmental screening tests are preventive, not remedial. By triggering in-depth assessment, screening instruments help teachers and other professionals decide who needs additional support for learning, rather than potentially being used to judge whether classrooms are meeting standards set from the outside.

In addition to **developmental screening tests** and **achievement tests,** the other principal types of tests that are useful to early childhood educators are:

- **social-emotional/behavioral screening tests**—brief assessments that focus on aspects of social-emotional development specifically, rather than on development in general; some assessments look strictly at behavior problems and don't assess the full range of social and emotional (or "affective") development
- **readiness tests**—brief achievement tests that seek to determine a child's relative preparedness to participate in a particular classroom program
- **instructional assessments**—assessments based on children's actual classroom performance that are intended to guide a teacher's instructional decision making and monitor children's progress

Among additional tests administered in early childhood are **diagnostic assessments,** which are used to determine a child's specific areas of strength or weakness. Diagnostic assessments are typically performed by specialists, and are discussed elsewhere in this guide.

As this guide explains, all these tests differ significantly from one another and should never be used interchangeably—particularly screening and readiness tests. Both screening tests and readiness tests have roles to play in early childhood programs. But they serve different purposes. Unlike screening tests, readiness tests are not very good at making predictions about children's school success.

It is extremely important that tests not be used to make high-stakes decisions in early childhood programs. "High-stakes" tests are those directly linked to decisions regarding children's entry into a program or promotion or retention, that are used for evaluating or rewarding teachers or administrators, that affect the allocation of resources to programs, and that result in changes in the curriculum. Because children's development, and therefore their performance on any test, is so variable in their early childhood years, none of those "high-stakes" decisions should be based solely or primarily on test scores. Rather, tests should only provide supplementary information to help the teacher, parent, and other specialists arrive at the best possible decision for each child.

Experience has taught us that we must never remove ourselves from the process of assessment to rely on tests alone to make important decisions about children's lives. Testing is not a natural environment, particularly for young children. Whenever possible, we should use test data in conjunction with information from parents, teachers, other professionals, and firsthand observations of children.

The place where all of this begins is with developmental screening. This guide defines screening and distinguishes it from other kinds of assessments. It tells how to evaluate tools that meet basic criteria of statistical (or "psychometric") acceptability. And it presents many practical details of mounting and implementing a screening program.

Finally, the guide describes the limitations of screening. All tests, including screening instruments, have important restrictions. If we could do a better job of recognizing the limitations of the assessments that children encounter in their school careers we might be in a better position to remember that tests should never be the masters of the educational process. At best, they can facilitate that process.

Chapter 1

Purpose of Developmental Screening

What is early childhood developmental screening?

Screening is a brief assessment procedure designed to identify children who, because they might have a learning problem or disability, should receive more extensive assessment. A simple example might be a vision test: If a child had difficulty passing a vision screening test, this should trigger the child being sent to an optometrist or ophthalmologist for examination and diagnosis.

Some organized preschool programs provide children with screening routinely. Some children, especially those not in organized programs, may come to screening through "childfind" activities—that is, activities that make families aware of the availability of screening, diagnosis, and intervention services.

Early childhood screening occurs early in a child's preschool experience. It serves as the first step in a prevention, evaluation, and intervention process that is intended to help children achieve their potential. Screening is performed to identify children who might profit from early educational intervention or from special services in preschool or Head Start or before kindergarten or first grade. Developmental screening tests (or "instruments") briefly survey a young child's abilities in language, reasoning, gross motor, fine motor, and personal/social development to determine quickly and efficiently whether that child should undergo further assessment and evaluation. **Appendix 1** provides detailed information about the following well-known screening instruments:

- Ages & Stages Questionnaires: A Parent-Completed, Child-Monitoring System, 2nd Ed. (ASQ)
- AGS Early Screening Profiles
- Denver II
- Developmental Indicators for the Assessment of Learning-3rd Ed. (DIAL-3); Speed DIAL (short-form version)
- Early Screening Inventory·Revised (ESI·R)
- First Screening Test for Evaluating Preschoolers (FirstSTEp)

The screening process should incorporate information from multiple sources. In addition to developmental screening instruments, information about children should be collected from medical examinations, hearing and vision tests, and parent questionnaires and interviews.

Children identified by screening as possibly having developmental or learning problems or disabilities should receive further evaluation—typically termed "diagnostic assessment"—performed by one or more specialists. If indicated by the results of the diagnostic assessment, such children should receive specific intervention or remediation.

Figure 1 presents the sequence in which these identification, assessment, and intervention procedures take place.

Why screen?

Developmental screening helps schools meet the federal obligation of the Individuals with Disabilities Education Act (IDEA; recently reauthorized as the Individuals with Disabilities Education Improvement Act of 2004) to find, identify, and serve children with disabilities. In addition, all Head Start programs are required to

Figure 1. Sequence of identification, assessment, and intervention events

Purpose	Typical Activities	Persons Involved
Childfind		
To locate and make families aware of the availability of screening	census taking, newspaper and media publicity, posters, leaflets, referrals	state personnel, school staff, volunteers, community members, health care professionals
Screening		
To identify children who may have developmental or learning problems or disabilities	administration of screening instruments, medical exams, hearing and vision tests; completion of parent questionnaires; direct observation	teachers, other professionals, parents, paraprofessionals
Diagnostic Assessment		
To determine whether the child actually has a disability/problem, and if so what type; to propose possible remediation strategies	formal evaluations, parent conferences, evaluation team meetings	educators, psychologists, parents, clinicians, physicians, social workers
Individual Program Planning		
To develop an individual educational plan (IEP), program placement, and curriculum activities for the child	classroom observation, informal evaluation, development of instructional objectives	teachers, parents, evaluation team personnel, other professionals

provide developmental screening within 45 days of each child's enrollment. Other early care and education settings (e.g., state pre-K, public kindergartens, Title XX child care) may or may not have requirements to perform screenings. But, regardless of formal requirements, all programs should consider establishing a screening program because it is of potential value to young children.

A primary rationale for screening is prevention—to help children who need services gain access to them at a very early stage in order to prevent the occurrence of more severe problems later. Many chronic conditions, such as vision and hearing problems, are characterized by "silent periods" when symptoms are not yet apparent. Screening serves as a means for uncovering these conditions during the silent period, or at least when the problems or delays first become apparent, so intervention can be started while the probability of remediation is still high and before other problems accumulate.

Young children's development is characterized by peaks and plateaus rather than a smooth, steady increase in ability. In addition, children's continued development is influenced by the ability of the environment to support the next levels of development. Therefore, screening should occur at regular intervals during the first five years of life. Problems not evident at one time may appear later.

In general, developmental screening is based on the premise that a young child's skills, abilities, and achievements are not fixed or immutable. For example, studies demonstrate that early childhood intervention programs can significantly alter the course and developmental potential of many children who are at risk because of a learning problem or disability during their early years of life. By helping a child obtain early intervention services, developmental screening contributes to the eventual reduction in the number of children who experience school failure and dropout, and who may need special services in later years (Bowman, Donovan, & Burns 2001; Schweinhart, Barnes, & Weikart 1993; Shonkoff & Meisels 2000; Shonkoff & Phillips 2000).

What is the EPSDT program?

The Early and Periodic Screening, Diagnosis, and Treatment Program (EPSDT) was created in 1967 as an amendment to the federal Medicaid law. It requires that every state that operates a Medicaid program provide free periodic health and developmental screening, diagnosis, and treatment to all Medicaid-eligible children younger than 21 years of age. Medical, vision, hearing, and dental screening are all included. The medical screen calls for a comprehensive health and developmental history plus assessment of both physical and mental health.

EPSDT was designed to provide publicly funded comprehensive assessment and intervention services to the children of low-income families and/or to individuals with disabilities. In practice, however, the program has been beset by administrative and political problems of such magnitude that many eligible children are not screened.

Developmental screening—particularly for children younger than age 6—is a mandated service under EPSDT. The providers of such services, either private practitioners or departments of public health, welfare, or social services, and the actual procedures used vary according to state regulations. All children with Medicaid-eligible families are entitled to these services. Although the potential of EPSDT has never been realized, it is a resource that should be explored for children in need. Local departments of public health can provide information about how to take greater advantage of this potentially valuable program.

What does a developmental screening test consist of?

Developmental screening instruments focus on a wide range of child development domains, specifically speech, language, cognition, perception, affect, and gross and fine motor. Screening tests that address only one of these areas, or that exclude several areas, have the potential to overlook or lead to misidentification of children with problems in those areas.

In addition to such *general* developmental domains, children's behavioral or social-emotional development should also be screened specifically. Screening of social-emotional development will be discussed in **Chapter 2**. A number of measures have been developed in this area; **Appendix 2** provides detailed information about several.

Individual screening tests differ. But most items on general developmental screening tests can be grouped as follows:

- **Visual-motor/adaptive**—items that examine such aspects of fine motor control as eye-hand coordination and the ability to remember visual sequences, draw two-dimensional visual forms, and reproduce three-dimensional visual structures.
- **Language and cognition**—items that focus on language comprehension; verbal expression and articulation; and the abilities to reason, count, and to remember and repeat auditory sequences.
- **Gross motor/body awareness**—items that examine balance, gross motor coordination, and the ability to imitate body positions from visual cues.

These items are typically administered one-to-one (examiner and child) in a game-like situation using manipulatives, questions directed by the examiner to the child, and opportunities for the child to move around and respond. Some screening tests also ask children to draw a picture of a person—a man or a woman, a boy or a girl. This permits an examiner to better understand how a child organizes a response to a relatively unstructured request and also how the child represents a human figure pictorially.

In addition to the standardized information provided by the developmental screening instrument, a great deal of observational data about the child can be gained from the screening. **Figure 2** describes some of the information a careful examiner can collect during the administration of a screening test.

Figure 2. Observations that can be made during screening that may signal a developmental problem

In addition to the standardized information provided by developmental screening instruments, a great deal of observational data about the child can be collected from the screening. Careful administrators will gather as many observations as possible about a child during screening so the hypotheses they develop during that process can be confirmed or eliminated by subsequent interactions with the child.

Vision or hearing

Child rubs eyes, holds head near paper, says "what?" frequently, misunderstands words, turns or tilts head to hear; has one eye that crosses or wanders, has red eyes

Social-emotional behavior

Child is very shy, unusually willful; refuses or withdraws; tells frightening or bizarre stories

Information processing

Child needs instructions repeated often; is very distractible or unable to move on to the next task; does not monitor own performance; examines work overly carefully

Language development

Child mispronounces sounds, is unintelligible overall, uses immature syntax or impoverished or rambling expressive language

Fine motor

Child grips pencil awkwardly, makes jerky movements, switches hands during pencil tasks

Gross motor

Child has peculiar gait—stiff or jerky, toe walks, waves hands during balancing

Other sources of information

Watch the parent and child together to see whether the parent appears concerned? angry? uninterested? relaxed?

Ask the parent whether the child's performance was unusual? as expected?

Analyze the parent questionnaire for information about prenatal and perinatal history, illness, and opinions of child's temperament and abilities

Adapted from: S.J. Meisels & D.B. Marsden. 1997. *Trainer's Manual for the Early Screening Inventory·Revised.* New York: Pearson Early Learning.

Chapter 2

Scope of Developmental Screening

How does developmental screening differ from diagnostic assessment?

Screening is a limited procedure. Screening can indicate only that a child *might* have a problem that should be further investigated. It cannot definitively confirm the presence of the problem nor describe the nature and extent of a disability. Screening must be followed by further diagnostic assessment in order to confirm or refute any suspicions that the screening raises about a child. Thus, screening tests are used to select children who *might* have special needs.

In contrast, diagnostic assessment is a process used to identify definitively those children who *do* have special needs. Diagnostic assessments probe more deeply within developmental areas. These assessments are lengthier than a screening; some are administered over a period of several days or weeks.

Screening thus represents a threshold children must pass to avoid being subject to further evaluation. However, it is important to remember that tests do not have magical powers. Even if a child passes the screening hurdle, further evaluation is warranted whenever a teacher or parent has evidence that the child is having difficulty functioning well in the daily routine. Children who have obvious or severe handicapping conditions need not be screened; such children, who are already identified as having a disability, need to participate in the evaluation process only.

The purposes of diagnostic assessment are to identify a child's specific areas of strength and weakness; determine the nature of a child's problems; suggest the cause of the problem or deficiency, if possible; and make general recommendations about suitable remediation strategies. To achieve these goals, diagnostic assessments should be performed by a multidisciplinary team of professionals and utilize multiple methods for gathering information such as tests, observations, interviews, and parent reports.

Examples of diagnostic assessment instruments that can be used with young children include the following:

• Battelle Developmental Inventory-2nd Ed. (BDI-2; Riverside Publishing)

• Kaufman Assessment Battery for Children (K-ABC; AGS Publishing)

• McCarthy Scales of Children's Abilities (MSCA; Psychological Corporation)

• Merrill-Palmer-Revised Scales of Development (Merrill-Palmer-R; Psychological Assessment Resources, Inc.)

• Wechsler Preschool and Primary Scale of Intelligence-III (WPPSI-III; Psychological Corporation)

In addition to these instruments, there are also many diagnostic assessments that probe particular domains of development, such as language or motor development. They provide one-on-one opportunities for the examiner to evaluate a child's skills, knowledge, and abilities by, for example, asking the child to respond to questions, complete puzzles, point to words that are spoken, repeat digits or sounds, or hop, skip, balance, or throw a ball or beanbag.

Figure 3 represents the relationship of an early screening program to comprehensive assessment and intervention services.

Figure 3. Relationship of an early screening program to comprehensive assessment and intervention services

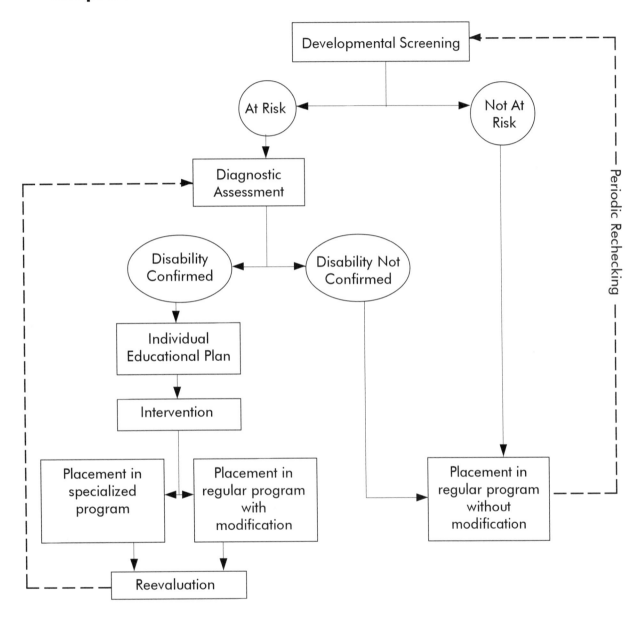

Only a diagnostic assessment process, not screening, should be used to label children, assign them to particular programs, or develop specific intervention procedures. It is only through comprehensive assessment and evaluation in a multidisciplinary setting that the existence of a disabling condition can be determined definitively, an individual educational plan (IEP) can be developed, and the most appropriate intervention/remediation services can be specified.

How does developmental screening differ from readiness testing?

Developmental screening tests and readiness tests serve different purposes and measure different sets of skills and abilities. The major difference between the two procedures lies in the distinction between the *ability or potential* to acquire skills and current skill

acquisition. Developmental screening tests focus on the process whereby children acquire skills. Readiness tests focus on what actual skills children have acquired.

Readiness tests are used for group placement and curriculum planning. They are designed to identify a child's relative preparedness for benefiting from a specific academic program. Readiness tests focus on a child's current skill achievement and performance relative to the requirements of a particular curriculum—that is, what does the child know and what is she/he able to do as a foundation for future learning. Thus, a child's poor performance on a readiness test may indicate only a lack of general knowledge or experience. For example, a child may not be able to cut out a circle with scissors, but this may be because he has never had the opportunity to use scissors, not because he is incapable or impaired in his motor ability.

In contrast, developmental screening instruments identify children who may have a learning problem or handicapping condition that could affect their potential for learning. Although a child's performance on a screening instrument is influenced by that child's general experience and knowledge, screening tests also include items that do not measure particular achievements or experiences. A screening test might, for example, measure auditory or visual sequential memory (remembering sights or sounds presented in a particular sequence).

Because screening and readiness tests provide different but valuable information, they should be used to complement, rather than substitute for, each other.

Well-known examples of readiness tests include the following:

- Boehm Test of Basic Concepts-3rd Ed. (Boehm-3; Psychological Corporation)
- Bracken Basic Concept Scale-Revised (BBCS-R; Psychological Corporation)
- Brigance K & 1 Screen-II (Curriculum Associates, Inc.)
- Cognitive Skills Assessment Battery (CSAB; Teachers College Press)

- Metropolitan Readiness Tests, 6th Ed. (MRT 6; Psychological Corporation)
- Stanford Early School Achievement Test (SESAT; Harcourt)

Can we screen for social-emotional development?

Screening for problems related to children's social-emotional (or "affective") development—mood, temperament, social problem solving, personality, self-concept, self-regulation—is very difficult to do accurately. Screening is a brief assessment and usually takes place before the child and the examiner have had an opportunity to get to know each other well. The absence of a personal relationship between the child and the examiner can have a greater impact on the evaluation of behavior or affect than is the case with the screening of cognitive, language, or physical development. As a result, it is very challenging to identify possible emotional problems in young children without spending a lot of time with them.

Rather than utilizing direct assessment by examiners, most screens of social-emotional development ask families to supply information about their children (termed "parent report"). It is important to be aware, however, that children may act differently with their family members and in the comfort of their homes than they do in Head Start, preschool, kindergarten, or other early childhood settings. In short, emotional development is very susceptible to environmental influences. The behaviors a child shows may not concern his or her family, but that child could still be at risk for emotional issues at school because the social demands of school might elicit quite different behaviors than home might. Alternatively, children may function well within the structure of a school environment, but have great difficulty in the relatively unstructured environments outside of school.

This is an area that will always require sensitive and careful collaboration between the school and the home. Despite the challenges of assessing this domain, the importance of social-emotional competence to children's future outcomes requires that we carefully monitor development in this domain.

Several of the available screening instruments in this area have acceptable statistical properties (see **Appendix 2** for reviews). Examples of screens of social-emotional development include the following:

- Ages & Stages Questionnaires: Social Emotional (ASQ:SE; Brookes Publishing)
- Devereux Early Childhood Assessment (DECA; Kaplan Early Learning Company)
- Early Screening Project (ESP; Sopris West)
- Preschool and Kindergarten Behavior Scales-2nd Ed. (PKBS-2; Pro-Ed)
- Temperament and Atypical Behavior Scale (TABS; Brookes Publishing)

Chapter 3

Selecting a Screening Instrument

What are test reliability and validity?
Why are they essential?

Developmental screening tests should be reliable and valid. Tests that do not have well-established statistical (or "psychometric") characteristics should be avoided or used only with great caution.

Reliability is a statistical indicator of how consistently or how often identical test results can be obtained with the same screening instrument. It is a formal measure of our confidence that a test will assess the same thing (a skill, achievement, behavior, etc.) when it is used repeatedly by different examiners with different children.

Reliability studies are performed by test developers or researchers (see citations in **Appendixes 1 and 2**) on test instruments to determine the extent to which fluctuations in the test results are due to chance or to factors unrelated to that which is being assessed. For example, using a reliable instrument means that if one child receives a high score and another a low score on a screen for gross motor, we can be confident that the difference in scores is attributable to differences in the two children's gross motor development, not to some random factor like the way a test question is phrased or the materials used.

Several types of reliability are reported for screening instruments, including *interobserver reliability, test-retest reliability,* and *internal reliability.* Generally, correlations that show agreement above 80 percent are considered acceptable in reliability studies. (See **Appendix 3** for a more technical discussion of how reliability is determined.)

Validity tells us whether a test is measuring what we want to measure and not something altogether different. Reliability is one measure of internal validity; so reliability is necessary in order for a test to be valid, but it is not enough.

Validity is a statistical indicator of the accuracy of the inferences that can be drawn from a test. In other words, the stronger the validity of these inferences, the more believable are the test's results. Knowledge of test validity is essential, because it allows the user to evaluate how well the test accomplishes its stated purpose. Validity data should be collected by test developers and researchers and published in test manuals and professional journals (see citations in **Appendixes 1 and 2**). Screening tests with unknown or poor validity data should not be used.

Validity is inherently relative: It is determined by comparing, correlating, or contrasting findings with some other index, criterion, or construct. In one aspect of validity, screening test results can be compared with the results of a diagnostic assessment. Validity is then inferred from the strength of association between findings identified in screening and the presence of the actual condition as confirmed by the diagnostic assessment.

For example, if children identified by a certain screening instrument as being at risk for fine motor problems are consistently found through in-depth diagnostic assessment to actually have fine motor problems, then that screen is valid. That is, we can infer that it is measuring what we want it to measure. By contrast, a test that purported to measure fine motor skills that was administered in English to children who spoke only Vietnamese would in fact be measuring language skills, not motor skills. The results from such an administration would not be valid.

Screening instruments often report both *concurrent validity* and *predictive validity*. Some screening tests report data in terms of *face validity* (sometimes called "content validity"), which, rather than being statistical in nature, represents the independent judgment of professionals concerning the relevance of the items of a screening instrument. In general, valid inferences from screening tests require that at least 80 percent of those at-risk and not at-risk be correctly identified. See **Appendix 3** for a more technical discussion of how validity is determined.

If no measures of reliability and validity are available from the manual or research literature concerning a screening instrument, we cannot be confident that its results are not random or inaccurate. Given that the purpose of screening is to maximize the correct identification of children at risk, it is essential that only valid instruments be used.

Screening that misidentifies children as needing further assessment when they really don't (termed "over-referral") is expensive and can burden the school district or individuals responsible for providing diagnostic assessments. In addition, misidentification can negatively alter the parents' perception of their child by inappropriately suggesting problems or difficulties that are not really there. In contrast, not identifying children who really could benefit from services ("under-referral") denies children who need help the opportunity to receive it and defeats the purpose of screening.

What decisions must be made when planning a developmental screening program?

A variety of issues should be considered and a number of specific decisions must be made in planning a developmental screening program.

Who will administer the instrument? Some instruments are designed to be administered by teachers or psychologists and some by paraprofessionals. Because subjective judgment usually plays a role in assessing a child's overall performance, it is important that the person who administers the screening has some understanding of, and background in, child development.

Will the instrument be administered to individual children, or will it be given to a group of children? Screening instruments should be administered to individual children. Although some screening items may lend themselves to a group approach, administering a screening instrument to a group will probably result in a greater proportion of children's problems going undetected. Best practice calls for administering all early childhood assessments individually.

Is the instrument reliable and valid? If the instrument is not known to be reliable and valid, the accuracy of the inferences based on the instrument is unknown. Unless the reliability and validity data of a screening instrument are reported with the instrument, the results of the screening may be misleading. Tests that don't report reliability and validity data should not be used.

Are normative scores available on a population similar to yours? Statistically standard scores (called "normative" scores) are necessary in order to establish appropriate cutoff points for referrals—that is, in order to establish what scores on the screen should trigger diagnostic assessment. These cutoffs may vary for children who are raised in contexts different from the sample of children used to standardize the assessment. This is where validation of norms on local samples may be needed; for more on conducting validity studies, see **Appendix 3.**

Is the instrument available in more than one language, and is it fair to children from different cultures? Children who do not speak English as their primary language or whose family culture differs from the mainstream should not be penalized by the limitations of the screening instrument. Select an instrument that is suited to the child's language and background.

How long will screening take? Screening instruments should be brief. Just 15 to 20 minutes is the average time limit for screening a preschool or kindergarten child. Children below age 4 will probably require more time—perhaps 30 minutes.

How old are the children who are to be screened? Screening instruments are normed for specific age ranges. Be certain that the children you wish to screen are included in the age range covered by your screening instrument.

Is the screening test experience pleasant for most children? Because the same test is given individually to a large number of

Developmental Screening

children, and because screening must be completed in a brief time period, it is important that the test items be enjoyable, easily understood, and interesting enough so that each child's best performance can be elicited quickly.

Is there a parent questionnaire? Some screening instruments include a parent questionnaire as part of the screening procedure. The family is often in the best position to provide essential information about the child being screened. Questionnaires should be designed to elicit medical and developmental information in a simple, straightforward fashion. It is helpful for an examiner to see the completed questionnaire prior to screening the child, so the examiner can focus on the areas of concern identified by the parents. Some screening instruments rely solely on parent report. The wording of such questionnaires should probe both positive and negative behaviors. It is important to help families identify areas of their child's strengths as well as areas of concern. See **Appendix 4** for a sample parent questionnaire.

Is it difficult to learn how to administer and score the instrument? Screening instruments are usually administered individually to large numbers of children by multiple examiners. It should be possible to learn easily how to administer a screening instrument after studying the manual, watching an experienced examiner, and practicing under supervision with several children. All examiners must practice before administrating the instrument in a screening context. The scoring should be straightforward and easily interpretable.

Is the instrument expensive, or does it use costly apparatus? In general, screening should be efficient and inexpensive. Most screening instruments require a modest expenditure for manuals and equipment, plus the cost of consumable supplies such as score sheets and parent questionnaires.

Are the screening procedures acceptable to the specialists who will perform the follow-up assessment? If the instrument is statistically valid and reliable, if the examiners are well trained and supervised, and if the focus of the screening test is broad enough to provide an overall picture of the child's functioning, the results of the screening instrument should be acceptable to those administering the follow-up assessment. If any of these conditions are not met, the entire screening effort may be wasted.

Appendix 1 includes information that answers many of these questions about several commonly used screening instruments. The decision matrix shown on pages 29–30 can be duplicated and used when comparing screening instruments.

What criteria should be used in selecting screening instruments?

A developmental screening instrument must be able to meet general criteria in order to be used with confidence. An instrument must:

1. Be a brief procedure designed to identify children who may have a learning problem or disability that could affect their overall potential for success in school;

2. Consist of items that primarily sample the domain of developmental tasks, rather than children's specific academic readiness accomplishments;

3. Address several areas of development including speech, language, cognition, perception, social, emotional, and gross and fine motor; and

4. Provide information about how the test was developed and standardized, its normative characteristics, and its reliability and validity.

The first criterion is the general definition of developmental screening. The second criterion reflects the distinction between school readiness tests and developmental screening instruments. The

Evaluating an early childhood developmental screening instrument

Name of **screening instrument:** _____

_____

Authors of screening instrument: _____

_____

_____

The **age range** covered by the test is: _____

The instrument is designed to be **administered to:**

❒ individuals

❒ groups

The amount of time required for administration is _____ minutes.

The test can be **administered by:**

❒ teachers   ❒ parents

❒ specialists   ❒ volunteers/assistants

The following **training materials** are available:

❒ audiovisual materials: _____

❒ other: _____

The **developmental areas** covered by the test include:

❒ expressive language   ❒ auditory reception   ❒ perceptual-motor

❒ receptive language   ❒ gross motor   ❒ social

❒ reasoning   ❒ fine motor   ❒ emotional

❒ other _____

Description: _____

_____

_____

_____

_____

_____

The following **statistical information** is available:

standardized norms

❏ by age   ❏ by sex   ❏ other _____

reliability

interobserver = _____

test-retest = _____

validity

concurrent = _____ (correlation with: _____)

predictive = _____ (correlation with: _____)

sensitivity = _____ (criterion: _____)

specificity = _____ (criterion: _____)

The instrument provides for **parent input** through:

❏ parent questionnaire   ❏ parent report items   ❏ parent interview

The **languages,** other than English, in which it is available:

❏ Spanish   ❏ other _____

The **cost** of the test is:

Manual, materials, and scoresheets: $_____ for _____ children

The instrument is **available from:** _____

_____

Comments:_____

_____

_____

_____

_____

_____

_____

_____

third concerns the range of content that should be covered; and the last criterion highlights the importance of using screening tests that satisfy objective psychometric properties.

Should we use screens of individual areas of development?

With mounting attention by policy makers to academic domains such as literacy and mathematics, screening of individual areas of development is becoming more frequent. Numerous screens exist that focus on single domains such as language, motor, and cognition.

If single-domain screening is utilized, such instruments should not be used in isolation from a broader developmental screening such as those described in **Appendix 1.** Without information concerning children's other areas of development, it is possible to draw misleading conclusions about them. For example, a parent might report that her child does not follow directions and that she considers him a behavior problem. But hearing and speech-language items in a general developmental screening might show that the child has difficulty hearing, understanding, or remembering complex directions. Cognitive items might indicate problems with his understanding basic directional concepts, and motor items might indicate that he has difficulty with motor planning and cannot correctly sequence or execute complex movements on demand. Only after information about all domains of his development is collected from more than one source can valid hypotheses be made about his possible problems.

In recent years, screening measures have been developed to identify children who are at risk for reading failure (e.g., "Get Ready to Read!" [NCLD 2001] or "DIBELS" [University of Oregon 2004]). These measures focus more on letter and sound identification and phonemic awareness skills than on the overall language skills of children. And they do not take into account other variables such as family factors that are highly correlated with reading failure (Snow, Burns, & Griffin 1998). Such narrowing of focus in screening measures is of great concern given what we know about the interdependence of developmental domains. Such measures should not be used in the absence of broader developmental screening.

Chapter 2 includes a discussion of screening for social-emotional/behavioral problems. With social and emotional skills, it is especially important that screening (and diagnostic assessment) use multiple methods and multiple sources of information. Again, such screening should be done *in addition to* general developmental screening. One area particularly that has seen increased development of screening instruments is the identification of children with pervasive developmental disorders or autism. Because many of those instruments focus on identification before age 3 and this book is focused on the preschool years, such instruments are not reviewed here.

Should you design your own screening instrument?

The goals of developmental screening can be achieved only with screening tests that are valid. Most tests developed locally are not valid. Regardless, a survey of one state showed that more than 30 percent of the districts that responded were using locally developed screening tests comprising various subtests from standardized measures and other locally developed items with unknown validity (Costenbader, Rohrer, & DiFonzo 2000).

Screening tests should be used only if they meet acceptable professional criteria of standardization, reliability, and validity (American Educational Research Association, American Psychological Association, & National Council on Measurement in Education 1999). It is essential that sound evidence be available from test developers in their manuals or from published research studies that demonstrates that the sample of children with whom the test was developed included children similar to those who will be screened (in particular, in relation to children's cultural and socioeconomic backgrounds); that different examiners can obtain similar results if they give the test to the same child at different times (i.e., reliability); and that the inferences based on the test scores are accurate (i.e., validity). If these criteria are not satisfied, recommendations made about children based on the test should be treated with extreme caution.

Use of screening instruments that do not undergo a systematic test development phase can lead to the misidentification of children at risk, can result in unnecessary expenditures of time and money by schools, and can cause avoidable anxiety for families and their children. Just as we would not utilize screening measures with unknown accuracy as indicators of our physical health, so we should not use screens for developmental status that lack a strong research foundation.

Chapter 4

Screening Follow-Up

What actions can be taken based on developmental screening?

Typically, screening instruments yield one of two outcomes: Either a child is referred for diagnostic assessment, or the child is considered to be functioning within the normal range of development, albeit with important variations. (See **Figure 4** on the next page for suggestions about interpreting screening results.) However, this restricted choice between *refer* and *OK* is occasionally insufficient. Some children simply do not fit into these categories.

Thus, a third category is possible: *rescreen*. There are many reasons to rescreen a child. First, young children's development is in flux; in fact, instability of development typically is more the case than not. Second, the parent might report that the child's behavior was atypical on the day of screening, or the child might have recently recovered from an illness; perhaps the child does well on all but the last section of a screening instrument; or the location where the screening took place might have been disrupted. A child also should be rescreened if the parent questionnaire (**Appendix 4**) indicates a problem that was not picked up in the initial screening.

Figure 4. Suggestions about interpreting screening results

Factors that should be considered when interpreting a child's score on a screening instrument:

Did the child just barely miss or earn points?

Were most points lost in one section or domain?

Do points lost across sections fall into a pattern (e.g., child experiences difficulty when tasks are presented verbally; difficulty sequencing information on visual or auditory sequential memory; or problems with instructions)?

Did the child just move into the next older age group? If so, review the ratings you would have used if the screening had taken place a few days sooner.

Making decisions about follow-up:

Does the information from various sources suggest a consistent interpretation and recommendation?

Is additional information needed in an area not specifically scored on the screening (i.e., vision, hearing, speech, medical, social/emotional adjustment)?

Have you consulted with the child's teacher about the child's competence with classroom activities and the child's behavior in a group?

Adapted from: S.J. Meisels & D.B. Marsden. 1997. *Trainer's Manual for the Early Screening Inventory·Revised.* New York: Pearson Early Learning.

However, another critical occasion for rescreening a child is when the child's performance on the initial screen is indeterminate, falling midway between the *OK* and the *refer* cutoffs. Such children, who display general (or "nonspecific") delays across several areas of development, should be rescreened with the same test about eight to 10 weeks later to determine whether the screening was accurate and whether further action—referral either for diagnostic assessment or for individualized classroom programming—should take place.

Families should be offered developmental guidance when their child's score falls in the *rescreen* category. Care should be taken when talking to families to describe developmental activities that address the area of potential concern rather than a specific task. For example, parents should be encouraged to provide opportunities for their child to "develop gross motor skills," instead of being urged to practice hopping, skipping, and balancing with their child. This is important because the items on a screening test are intended to sample behavior that is representative of children's development in a given domain. The capacity of a screening item (one that asks the child to hop, for example) to represent a broader range of developmental skills may be impaired if a child is given prolonged practice on a single task (on hopping, in this example) before being rescreened.

Can screening information be used for program planning?

Because screening tests are not diagnostic, no definitive conclusions can be drawn about the nature of a child's problems or about specific remediation strategies. Similarly, for children who perform well on screening, the test may not be comprehensive or challenging enough to inform classroom program planning accurately.

However, for children in the *rescreen* category—those who display mild, nonspecific delays in development—the data from

screening can be used to initiate an individualized/modified class-room program that focuses on the child's areas of strengths and areas of weakness. For example, a child who does not do well on the visual-motor tasks might be given more experience with fine motor and visual motor skills.

Such a decision to individualize a child's classroom program should be made only when the following conditions are met:

- The child is rescreened, and the second set of results corresponds to the initial screening results.
- The child's classroom teacher and parents are directly involved in the decision to initiate modified classroom programming.
- The child's progress is monitored throughout the year and is evaluated at the end of the first year of individualized programming.

These conditions mirror the pre-referral process described in the Individuals with Disabilities Education Act (IDEA) and are intended to evaluate response to intervention.

If the child does not show significant improvement in the course of the year, as determined by the teacher, parents, and other sources of data, the child should be referred for further assessment. **Figure 5** on the next page provides an example of a cycle of kindergarten developmental screening, referral, and intervention. A similar plan for preschool-age children can be devised, particularly relying on parental participation.

The plan for modifying the child's classroom program should be developed by the child's teacher, preferably with the assistance of an early childhood resource teacher or consultant. The child's family should be involved in the decision to initiate modified programming and should also be included in the planning process. The results from screening can help focus a teacher's observations and organize her or his perceptions regarding a child, but those screening results are not intended to take the place of further ongoing classroom-based evaluation performed by the teacher.

Figure 5. A cycle of screening/rescreening, referral, and intervention

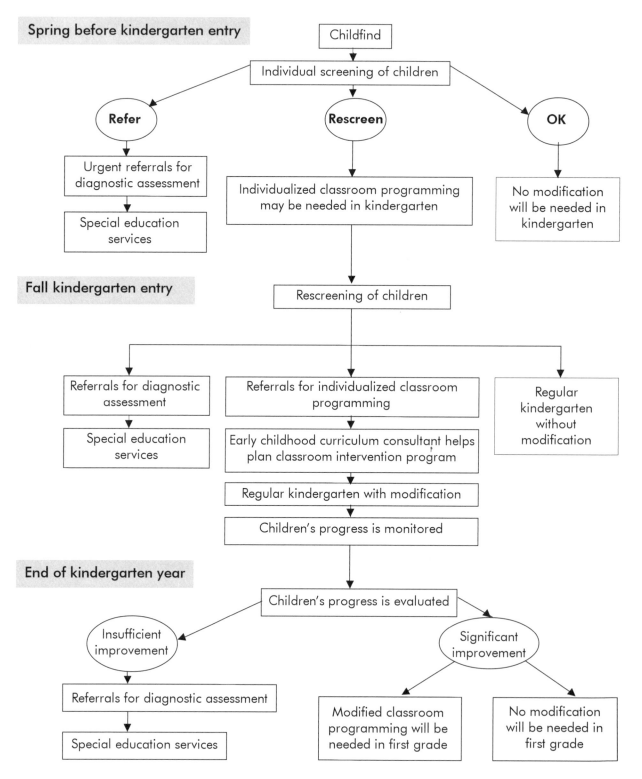

Spring before kindergarten entry

Childfind

Individual screening of children

Refer

Rescreen

OK

Urgent referrals for diagnostic assessment

Special education services

Individualized classroom programming may be needed in kindergarten

No modification will be needed in kindergarten

Fall kindergarten entry

Rescreening of children

Referrals for diagnostic assessment

Special education services

Referrals for individualized classroom programming

Early childhood curriculum consultant helps plan classroom intervention program

Regular kindergarten with modification

Children's progress is monitored

Regular kindergarten without modification

End of kindergarten year

Children's progress is evaluated

Insufficient improvement

Significant improvement

Referrals for diagnostic assessment

Special education services

Modified classroom programming will be needed in first grade

No modification will be needed in first grade

Developmental Screening

It should be noted that the *rescreen* category is not a substitute for follow-up diagnostic assessment. Children who receive modified classroom programming because they fall into the *rescreen* category should not be labeled, nor should they be considered children with special needs. Rather, they are children who are apparently not developing in a typical fashion and who could probably benefit from individualized classroom attention. Providing them with modified classroom program thus delays the decision, or even avoids the need, to refer these children for further assessment for a limited period of time. However, if any suspicion arises that a child's development may be substantially delayed, she or he should be referred immediately for diagnostic assessment.

Chapter 5

Setting Up a Screening Program

What are the components of an early childhood screening program?

Each component of a screening program requires advance planning. Before a screening program can be initiated, several decisions and actions regarding these components must be taken. Among them are the following:

1. Establish sources of funding.
2. Identify a coordinator of screening.
3. Select a broad-based committee to assist in planning and implementing the screening program. Be sure to include individuals who will be involved in the follow-up diagnostic assessments.
4. Specify the purposes and objectives of the screening program.
5. Determine the population to be screened.
6. Select the screening instrument(s) and procedure(s) to be used.
7. Arrange for appropriate locations and timing for screening.
8. Coordinate medical examinations and vision and hearing tests with the screening.
9. Publicize to parents information about the purpose of screening and the schedules of orientation sessions.

10. Enlist the cooperation of parents and other community members in identifying children who are to be screened (i.e., childfind).

11. Select and train screening personnel.

12. Provide professional development training for preschool, kindergarten, and other early childhood teachers and child care providers.

Once the screening program is launched:

13. Request information from parents and teachers if appropriate (e.g., parent questionnaire and parental consent, if required).

14. Assess children's comprehensive physical status.

15. Administer the developmental screen to children.

16. Monitor all program components.

17. Interpret screening data

18. Communicate with parents regarding results of screening and any recommendations for follow-up.

19. Notify assessment teams about the need for follow-up on individual children.

20. Evaluate the effectiveness of the screening program.

All children who are referred by the screening should receive follow-up assessment and, if indicated, appropriate intervention/remediation. **Figure 6** on page 46 diagrams the screening components. In order to develop an effective screening program, each step illustrated in the flow chart should be considered carefully.

Should parents be included in the screening process?

Parental involvement is critical to the success of an early childhood developmental screening program, and their involvement in diagnostic assessments is mandated by many state laws and by IDEA. This involvement can be indirect or direct.

Indirect involvement begins when the family is informed of the availability of screening services during the childfind activities.

Parents should be told what a screening program consists of, what its rationale is, who will perform the screening, where and when it will take place, how confidentiality will be respected, and how results will be communicated. This information typically is transmitted by media announcements such as newspaper articles, PTA meetings, or flyers distributed throughout the community.

The rights and the sensitivities of families and their children must be carefully respected. For many, screening represents a first experience with early education and care providers. Long waiting lines, chaotic reception rooms, and indifferent or poorly informed personnel should be avoided. Also avoided should be such demeaning agricultural metaphors as "Kindergarten Roundup." Instead, screening should take place in an environment that is high in respect and professional competence and low in anxiety and confusion.

There is also an important role for *direct* participation by family members. Just as a parent taking a child to the pediatrician would not expect to be separated from that child during the exam, so a parent should not be expected to be isolated from the child during

Figure 6. The components of a screening program

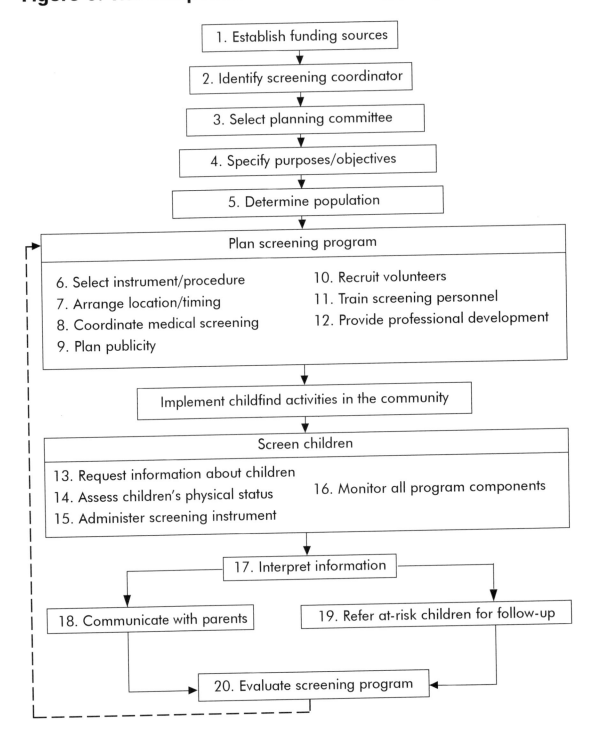

1. Establish funding sources
2. Identify screening coordinator
3. Select planning committee
4. Specify purposes/objectives
5. Determine population

Plan screening program

6. Select instrument/procedure
7. Arrange location/timing
8. Coordinate medical screening
9. Plan publicity
10. Recruit volunteers
11. Train screening personnel
12. Provide professional development

Implement childfind activities in the community

Screen children

13. Request information about children
14. Assess children's physical status
15. Administer screening instrument
16. Monitor all program components

17. Interpret information

18. Communicate with parents
19. Refer at-risk children for follow-up

20. Evaluate screening program

Developmental Screening

the developmental screening. Parents should be asked to accompany their children to the screening site. During the screening itself, they can be encouraged to sit near their child but out of the child's direct line of vision. Conversely, although all parents should be invited to attend screenings, no parent should be required to observe. In some cases, it is easier and less anxiety-provoking for parent and child to be separated for screening, and the discretion of the examiner and the parent should be used in making that decision.

Parents are also involved directly in screening when they complete a developmental screening parent questionnaire (**Appendix 4**). The questionnaire asks the parent or other family member to provide a history of the child's medical and developmental milestones, as well as signals problematic areas of development to the examiner. Finally, parents should receive direct feedback after the screening has been completed.

Parents whose children are developing typically should be informed of this promptly. If a child falls into the *rescreen* category or if the screening results trigger the child's referral for follow-up diagnostic assessment, the family should be contacted personally— in person, or by phone if a meeting can't be arranged. Screening yields only tentative results, and this fact should be clearly communicated to parents. The feedback should not make parents feel as if they have received a report card about their child. **Figure 7** on the next page offers some suggestions.

Screening should take place as early as possible and as soon as appropriate in a child's life. Moreover, screening should ideally occur while there is still opportunity for the child to benefit from early intervention, and before deficits become cumulative. The earlier screening takes place, the more time there is for the intervention system to meet the requirements of children found to have special needs.

Traditionally, the kind of early childhood screening and identification of developmental and learning problems that this book describes has taken place at the time of school entry, in the fall of the

Figure 7. Suggestions for discussing results of screening with parents

Remember that a screening test is not diagnostic. It can only indicate that further evaluation may be needed. Be sure to let the parents know this.

For children who do not do well on the screening, arrange for a meeting with the parents (or a phone conversation if a meeting is not possible).

Be supportive, and indicate what the child is doing well in addition to communicating things that puzzle or concern you.

Listen carefully to what the parents say. Work with them as a team to determine what is best for their child.

Be available for the parents to call you back with other questions after your meeting.

If you are going to make a referral for further evaluation, know what is available and whom to contact.

Express your concern, by asking the parents to be in touch with you after the evaluation.

Adapted from: S.J. Meisels & D.B. Marsden. 1997. *Trainer's Manual for the Early Screening Inventory•Revised*. New York: Pearson Early Learning.

Developmental Screening

child's kindergarten or first grade year, or sometimes in the spring before school entry. If screening takes place early, the child will have a greater likelihood of receiving prompt diagnostic assessment/evaluation and effective intervention.

The earlier the evaluation can occur as a result of earlier screening, the more lead time for planning and implementing necessary services for the child. The longer the lead time, the greater the period during which a child's learning problem can be corrected or compensated for. Screening should take place while there is still time to act effectively on the results of screening. Waiting too long can seriously reduce the possibility of effective remediation, as in cases of vision and hearing impairment.

Ideally, screening should begin in the infancy period and continue at periodic intervals throughout the early childhood period.

What expenses can be anticipated in establishing a screening program?

Several expenses should be expected when planning a screening program.

Finding children and publicizing the screening program (childfind). The community should be alerted to the availability of screening in a number of different ways. A letter and brochure sent home with all schoolchildren, notices in local newspapers, public service announcements on radio and television, and posters placed in supermarkets, laundromats, clinics, and other community locations are all helpful. These strategies are usually inexpensive yet effective. It is critical that this publicity be directed to *all* parents, not just those who suspect that their child might have special educational needs.

Purchasing the instrument. Enough copies of the screening instrument manual and materials should be obtained so that each examiner has her or his own set. This cost is usually not great, and should not be a recurring expense. Consumables, such as score sheets and parent questionnaires, must be purchased for all children who are to be screened each year, although some publishers grant permission to photocopy score sheets.

Administering the instrument. Included in this item are the costs to train personnel, administer the test, and monitor results.

Developmental Screening

This expense will vary according to the number of children to be screened, the method of administration, the number of examiners, and the flexibility of the examiners' time.

Following up the screening program. The costs involved in the follow-up of screening will be to record the screening results, analyze data, contact parents with results, facilitate referrals for further evaluation as appropriate, identify and contact those children absent for screening, locate children for rescreening, and set up parent conferences for children who appear to need further assessment.

Although the actual cost of screening may not be very great per child, follow-up and provision of diagnostic assessment and intervention/remediation services render screening the first step in a potentially expensive process. However, one of the fundamental assumptions of screening is that early identification and recognition of learning problems will, in many cases, lead to early remediation of disabilities. A cost-benefit analysis would therefore favor a greater expenditure at an early stage for a short period of time rather than increasingly larger expenditures in later years.

Chapter 6

Limitations of Developmental Screening

How predictive is developmental screening?

The screening instruments reviewed in **Appendix 1** have validity data available concerning their short- and long-term accuracy in predicting school performance. Nevertheless, the inferences drawn from these tests, when they are compared against one another, are not equally valid. Further, most screening instruments show a decline in accuracy of prediction over a period of two or more years—that is, they more accurately predict a child's developmental status near the time of screening, rather than what that child might be like several years down the road.

Many reasons might explain the declining accuracy of screening predictions over time. With the criteria that a developmental screening instrument must satisfy—brevity, efficiency, low cost, standardized administration, objective scoring, non-diagnostic focus, developmental content, validity measured by classificational rather than correlational methods—the possibility of high-level long-term predictive accuracy may be unattainable. In addition, children's development in their preschool years is not a smooth trajectory, often reflecting periods of rapid growth followed by integration of that growth or even temporary setbacks.

Put simply, developmental screening instruments are neither definitive nor comprehensive. They serve a very important purpose, but should be used only as indicators to alert parents and professionals to the need for more intensive follow-up assessment procedures. Those subsequent procedures should have a higher probability of being accurate and of supporting long-term prediction. Screening should never take place in isolation.

What are the limitations of early childhood screening instruments?

It is important to consider the limitations of screening so that the conclusions of a screening procedure are not distorted or misused. Many of the limitations, or potential abuses, of screening have been discussed in other sections of this book and are summarized below.

The data from screening should not be used as diagnostic/ assessment information. Screening only identifies potential problems. Diagnostic assessment is necessary to confirm or disconfirm this identification.

A screening instrument is not identical with a school entrance test. Developmental screening instruments are designed to find out whether a child may have some problem that will interfere with her or his acquisition of skills. In general, school entry or readiness tests seek to find out whether a child has acquired a certain minimum set of skills or body of knowledge that teachers need to know about in order to individualize instruction.

Screening tests are not IQ tests. IQ tests and screening instruments are not intended to be used for the same purposes. IQ scores are typically considered measures of a child's overall cognitive functioning. Screening instruments, by contrast, do not presume to reflect a child's entire range of cognitive functioning and should not be used as such. Often IQ tests are used in the diagnostic assessment component following screening.

Screening results should not be used to label a child. Terms such a "learning disabled," "mentally impaired," or "physically disabled" that refer to a child's intellectual, physical, or emotional status should be used only for well-defined purposes, if at all. No screening instrument is comprehensive enough to identify a child as having special needs. A screening test can begin to organize information about a child, but it should not be used for assigning diagnostic labels.

Screening instruments should not be used in multicultural/ multilingual communities if the instruments are not sensitive to cultural differences or the effects of bilingualism. Whenever possible, children should be screened in their native language. When a community serves families from a number of different cultures, the most appropriate screening instrument should be selected for each of these groups.

Screening should never be performed in isolation. It should always be performed within the context of a program of assessment, evaluation, and intervention. When an agency or school system establishes a screening program, it is committing itself to a process that can lead to the early identification of developmental and learning problems. The sponsoring organization has the moral responsibility to ensure that children who are identified by the process as being in need of special services receive follow-up assessment and intervention services. One must never lose sight of the overall context in which screening is performed.

References

American Educational Research Association, American Psychological Association, & National Council on Measurement in Education. 1999. *Standards for educational and psychological testing.* Washington, DC: American Educational Research Association.

Bowman, B.T., M.S. Donovan, & M.S. Burns, eds. 2001. *Eager to learn: Educating our preschoolers.* Washington, DC: National Academy Press.

Costenbader, V., A.M. Rohrer, & N. DiFonzo. 2000. Kindergarten screening: A survey of current practice. *Psychology in the Schools* 37 (4): 323–32.

Federal Interagency Forum on Child and Family Statistics. 2005. *America's children: Key national indicators of well-being, 2005.* Washington, DC: U.S. Government Printing Office. Online: http://childstats.gov/americaschildren/index.asp.

Filipek, P.A., et al. 2000. Practice parameter: screening and diagnosis of autism. Report of the quality standards subcommittee of the American Academy of Neurology and the Child Neurology Society. *Neurology* 55: 468–79.

NCLD (National Center for Learning Disabilities). 2001. *Get ready to read!* New York: Pearson Early Learning.

Schweinhart, L.J., H.V. Barnes, & D.P. Weikart. 1993. *Significant benefits: The High/Scope Perry Preschool study through age 27.* Ypsilanti, MI: High/Scope Press.

Shonkoff, J.P., & D.A. Phillips, eds. 2000. *From neurons to neighborhoods: The science of early childhood development.* Washington, DC: National Academy Press.

Shonkoff, J.P., & S.J. Meisels, eds. 2000. *The handbook of early childhood intervention.* 2d ed. New York: Cambridge University Press.

Snow, C.E., M.S. Burns, & P. Griffin, eds. 1998. *Preventing reading difficulties in young children.* Washington, DC: National Academy Press.

University of Oregon. 2004. *Dynamic Indicators of Basic Early Literacy Skills (DIBELS).* Online: http://dibels.uoregon.edu/.

U.S. Department of Health and Human Services. 1999. *Mental health: A report of the surgeon general.* Rockville, MD: U.S. Department of Health and Human Services, Substance Abuse and Mental Health Services Administration, Center for Mental Health Services, National Institutes of Health, National Institute of Mental Health. Online: www.surgeongeneral.gov/library/mentalhealth/home.html.

Bibliography

American Academy of Pediatrics Committee on Children with Disabilities. 2001. Developmental surveillance and screening of infants and young children. *Pediatrics* 108 (1): 192–96.

   This statement from the Committee focuses on the early identification of children with disabilities and makes recommendations concerning how pediatricians can participate in the screening process.

Barrera, I. 1996. Thoughts on the assessment of young children whose sociocultural background is unfamiliar to the assessor. In *New visions for developmental assessment of infants and young children*, eds. S.J. Meisels & E. Fenichel, 69–84. Washington, DC: Zero to Three: National Center for Infants, Toddlers, and Families.

   When assessors and families bring different world views, expectations, values, and behaviors to the assessment experience, screening and assessment become increasingly complex. This chapter explores dimensions of sociocultural diversity in relation to assessment and describes six steps to culturally responsive practice.

Brooks-Gunn, J., P.K. Klebanov, J. Smith, G.J. Duncan, & K. Lee. 2003. The black-white score gap in young children: Contributions of test and family characteristics. *Applied Developmental Science* 7 (4): 239–52.

   Examining black-white test score gaps in young children, the study found that demographic variables, family conditions, and home environment accounted for a large portion of the difference. Focusing on factors such as these that may be responsible for racial differences in test scores can help alter the way we interpret test results.

Buros Institute of Mental Measurements. 2005. *The sixteenth mental measurements yearbook*, eds. R.A. Spies & B.S. Plake. Lincoln, NE: Buros Institute of Mental Measurements.

The most comprehensive resource available on tests, this yearbook and its predecessors provide professional reviews of hundreds of tests in a number of different fields.

Horton, C., & B.T. Bowman. 2002. *Child assessment at the preprimary level: Expert opinion and state trends.* Occasional Paper of Herr Research Center. Chicago, IL: Erikson Institute. Online: www.erikson.edu/files/nonimages/horton-bowman.pdf.

Results of two surveys on the screening and assessment of young children are reported. One survey tapped the opinions of 25 national leaders regarding the components of high-quality assessment programs; the other surveyed state pre-K programs regarding specific assessment practices. Recommendations are provided.

Jablon, J.R., A.L. Dombro, & M.L. Dichtelmiller. 1999. *The power of observation.* Washington, DC: Teaching Strategies.

This is an excellent brief handbook about the uses of observation in assessment and teaching. It is very practical and useful for teachers of young children.

LaParo, K.M., & R.C. Pianta. 2000. Predicting children's competence in the early school years: A meta-analytic review. *Review of Educational Research* 70 (4): 443–84.

A meta-analysis of 70 longitudinal studies of school readiness, this report finds that predictions across time are relatively weak. The authors conclude that instability in early development as measured by these tests is more the rule than the exception.

Meisels, S.J. 1987, January. Uses and abuses of developmental screening and school readiness testing. *Young Children* 42: 4–6; 68–73.

This article describes the differences between developmental screening and school readiness testing. Focusing on the Gesell School Readiness Test, it describes some of the pitfalls of using tests for classification that are lacking adequate validity.

Meisels, S.J. 1999. Assessing readiness. In *The transition to kindergarten*, eds. R.C. Pianta & M.J. Cox, 39–66. Baltimore: Brookes Publishing.

Readiness is a difficult concept to define because of its fundamental relativity. It is even more difficult to assess. This chapter presents four different approaches to defining readiness and describes associated methods of assessment.

Meisels, S.J., & S. Atkins-Burnett. 2000. The elements of early childhood assessment. In *Handbook of early childhood intervention*, 2d ed., eds. J.P. Shonkoff & S.J. Meisels, 231–56. New York: Cambridge University Press.

This review chapter describes five elements of assessment: the target of assessment, the context in which assessments occur, limitations of conventional methods of assessment, varied roles of personnel in assessments, and the relationship of assessment to intervention.

O'Brien, J. 2001, April. How screening and assessment practices support quality disabilities services in Head Start. *Head Start Bulletin* 70. Online: www.headstartinfo.org/publications/hsbulletin70/hsb70_07.htm.

Describes appropriate strategies for screening and assessment in Head Start. Guidelines for screening and assessment are provided, as is a discussion of common pitfalls in screening. The article presents information for Head Start staff regarding communicating with parents about the results of screening.

Neisworth, J.T., & S.J. Bagnato. 1992. The case against intelligence testing in early intervention. *Topics in Early Childhood Special Education* 12 (1): 1–20.

Presents six misguided presumptions that underlie the use of intelligence tests with very young children. Concludes that assessment of young children is defensible only when it is tied to instruction or treatment.

Printz, P.H., A. Borg, & M.A. Demaree. 2003. *A look at social, emotional, and behavioral screening tools for Head Start and Early Head Start*. Boston, MA: Education Development Center, Inc. Online: http://notes.edc.org/CCF/ccflibrary.nsf/Libauthors?OpenView.

This document provides an overview of the Head Start Performance Standards regarding screening and a framework for choosing a specific screening tool. Descriptions are provided of six instruments that can be used for social-emotional screening.

Shepard, L.A., & M.L. Smith. 1986. Synthesis of research on school readiness and kindergarten retention. *Educational Leadership* 44: 78–86.

This is an extended discussion of the uses and misuses of school readiness testing and developmental screening. It provides important cautions based on research about how readiness tests can be used.

Wetherby, A., J. Woods, L. Allen, J. Cleary, H. Dickinson, & C. Lord. 2004. Early indicators of Autism Spectrum Disorders in the second year of life. *Journal of Autism and Developmental Disorders* 34 (5): 473–94.

This article discusses research that identified 13 red flags for identifying toddlers with autism and differentiating these toddlers from those who are typically developing or developmentally delayed. A correct classification rate of 94 percent was reported.

Also see

Early Childhood Research Institute on Culturally and Linguistically Appropriate Services (CLAS). *CLAS Special Collection—Evaluation tools.* Online: http://clas.uiuc.edu/special/evaltools/.

Descriptions of assessments, including screening instruments and assessments of bilingualism.

NAEYC. 2004, January. Resources on assessment. *Beyond the Journal.* Online: www.journal.naeyc.org/btj/200401/resources.asp.

Books and articles recommended by authors of articles published in *Young Children*'s January 2004 "Assessment" cluster.

Developmental Screening Instruments

During the past several decades, many instruments have been developed for early childhood screening. Very few of these instruments meet the selection criteria that are presented in this book, that an instrument should:

1. Be a brief procedure that identifies children at risk for learning problems or disabilities;

2. Focus on developmental tasks, rather than academic readiness tasks;

3. Sample a wide range of developmental areas;

4. Provide classificational data concerning the reliability and validity of the instrument.

The six instruments described in this appendix are individually administered developmental screening tests (not school readiness tests, intelligence tests, or tests of specific sensory or intellectual abilities) for preschool and kindergarten age children. Screening tests for children birth to 3 are not covered unless they also include forms for preschoolers. The screening tests reviewed here were developed or revised within the past 15 years. Most involve direct assessment of individual children. Although not all of the instruments meet the recommended guidelines for validity, information about them is included so readers can make evaluations and comparisons of well-known screening instruments. Please refer to **Appendix 3** for an explanation of technical terms, particularly *sensitivity* and *specificity*. Descriptions of additional screening instruments not reviewed in this appendix are found in several of the entries in the **Bibliography.**

Unless otherwise indicated, we obtained all information from the test manuals or publishers' Web sites. We strongly recommend a study of the screening manuals, score sheets, and materials for additional information.

Contents:

- Ages & Stages Questionnaires: A Parent-Completed, Child-Monitoring System, 2nd Ed. (ASQ)
- AGS Early Screening Profiles (ESP)
- Denver II
- Developmental Indicators for the Assessment of Learning-3rd Ed. (DIAL-3); Speed DIAL
- Early Screening Inventory·Revised (ESI·R)
- First Screening Test for Evaluating Preschoolers (FirstSTEp)

Ages & Stages Questionnaires: A Parent-Completed, Child-Monitoring System, 2nd Ed. (ASQ; 1999)

Authors: D. Bricker & J. Squires (with L. Mounts, L. Potter, R. Nickel, E. Twombly, & J. Farrell)

Age ranges: 4 months to 60 months

The amount of **time** for administration is 10–30 minutes.

The test is designed to be **administered** by parents (self-administered or by interview).

The following **training materials** are available:
- Detailed instructions
- Videotapes: administration, and scoring and referral

The **developmental areas** covered by the test:

The scales on the ASQ are communication, gross motor, fine motor, problem solving, and personal-social. The personal-social area addresses adaptive behavior (e.g., self-feeding, dressing) and interactions with others (e.g., how the child gets adult attention). There are 30 items on each illustrated questionnaire. In addition, the ASQ asks parents about the child's hearing, talking, movement, medical problems, and any concerns that the parents might have.

This instrument provides for **parent input** through: parent completion of the questionnaire or interview of parent.

The **languages** available other than English: Spanish, French, Korean, and Norwegian (Janson & Squires 2004). Mandarin and Arabic translations are under development.

The following **statistical information** is available:

Standardized norms are available for each of the 19 age interval forms.

Reliability

Interobserver	= 94% agreement (parents and examiner who assessed child)
Test-retest	= 94% agreement (two-week interval; same parent)

Validity

Concurrent	= 96% of the children with known disabilities scored below the cutoff score on the ASQ
Predictive	= N/A
Sensitivity	= .75 median across age groups*
Specificity	= .86 median across age groups

*Sensitivity ranges from .90 (36-month ASQ with the *Stanford-Binet* and *McCarthy*) to .51 (4-month ASQ with the *Revised Gesell Developmental Schedules*) across the different forms.

The total **cost** of the test is $190.

The total cost of the ASQ includes reproducible forms (questionnaires and summary sheets) and a user's guide including intervention activities.

The instrument is **available from:**

Brookes Publishing Co.
P.O. Box 10624
Baltimore, MD 21285-0624
www.brookespublishing.com
800-638-3775

Comments

Nineteen age-relevant questionnaires are available from 4 months to 60 months of age. Sample parent-child activities are available for each age range. All the questionnaires and scoring sheets as well as intervention activities are available on a CD-ROM.

The items are written at a fourth to sixth grade reading level, and many items are illustrated.

A database program (ASQ Manager) is available to help agencies compile and communicate results. Reports can be generated by child or by center. The reports can identify areas that may need further assessment and will generate a letter to parents about the child's screening results.

In an Australian study of premature infants using the previous edition of the ASQ (1995), only 67 percent of the children with known disabilities had ASQ overall scores that agreed with the psychometric assessment (Skellern, Rogers, & O'Callaghan 2001); however, the study reported overall sensitivity of .90, comparing the entire sample's assessment results using the 2 standard deviation cutoff on the ASQ and a below 1 standard deviation for the assessments. Solomon (2001) notes that while the ASQ is inexpensive and easy to use, "screening tests that offer more consistent scores are available." (Specifically mentioned are the *Early Screening Inventory. Revised* and the *Birth to Three Developmental Scale.*)

Supplementary Information

Janson, H., & J. Squires. 2004. Parent-completed developmental screening in a Norwegian population sample: a comparison with U.S. normative data. *Acta Paediatrica* 93 (11): 1525–29.

Singleton, D.M. 2001. Review of Ages and Stages Questionnaires. In *The fourteenth mental measurements yearbook,* eds. B.S. Plake & J.C. Impara, 49–50. Lincoln, NE: Buros Institute of Mental Measurements.

Skellern, C., Y. Rogers, & M.J. O'Callaghan. 2001. A parent-completed developmental questionnaire: Follow up of ex-premature infants. *Journal of Pediatric Child Health* 37: 125–29.

Solomon, R.H. 2001. Review of Ages and Stages Questionnaires. In *The fourteenth mental measurements yearbook,* eds. B.S. Plake & J.C. Impara, 50–51. Lincoln, NE: Buros Institute of Mental Measurements.

Squires, J., D. Bricker, & L. Potter. 1997. Revision of a parent-completed developmental screening tool: Ages & Stages Questionnaires. *Journal of Pediatric Psychology* 22 (3): 313–28.

Squires, J., D. Bricker, L. Potter, & S. Lamorey. 1998. Parent-completed developmental questionnaires: Effectiveness with low and middle income parents. *Early Childhood Research Quarterly* 13 (2): 345–54.

AGS Early Screening Profiles (ESP; 1990)

Authors: P. Harrison, A. Kaufman, N. Kaufman, R. Bruininks, J. Rynders, S. Ilmer, S. Sparrow, & D. Cicchetti

Age ranges: 2 years to 6 years, 11 months

The amount of **time** for administration is 15–40 minutes (with parent and teacher questionnaires of 10–15 minutes).

The instrument is designed to be **administered** individually by teachers or specialists.

The following **training materials** are available:
- Blackline masters in the manual
- Videotape

The **developmental areas** covered by the test:
> This instrument is composed of three profiles: cognitive/language, motor, and self-help/social. There are also four surveys: articulation, home, health history, and a behavior survey that is based on observations during the assessment. The authors suggest that individuals administer those portions of the instrument most applicable to their needs. The manual suggests that referrals may be made based on domain profiles (rather than the composite scores).

This instrument provides for **parent input** through: parent questionnaire.

The **languages** available other than English: none.

The following **statistical information** is available:
> *Standardized norms* by age were developed with a nationally representative sample of 1,149 children. Age level samples vary by age and scale with some smaller than 100 (Barnett 1995).

Reliability

Interobserver	= .80–.99 (reported for the motor scale)
Test-retest	= .84 (total screening and parent questionnaire composite; ranged from .56 to .82 for the domain screening indices)

Validity

Concurrent	= .76 (average correlation of domain screening index with comparable area in *Vineland Adaptive Behavior Scales*)
	= .66 (motor profile with *Bruininks-Oseretsky Battery*)
	= .68–.84 (cognitive and language domains with *Kaufman Assessment Battery for Children*)
Predictive	= .56 (Stanford Achievement after one year)
	= .56 (teacher grades in reading)
	= .37 (teacher grades in mathematics)
	= .58 (Otis-Lennon)
Sensitivity	= .53–.67*
Specificity	= .86–.88*

*Sensitivity and specificity are based on several studies that showed a range of percentages of children correctly referred. Harrison (personal communication 2004) stated that the variability in the sensitivity and specificity is most likely due to difference in criteria for special needs.

The total **cost** of the test is $384.99
   Score sheets: $81 for 25 children (if all profiles and surveys are administered).

The instrument is **available from:**
   AGS Publishing
   4201 Woodland Road
   Circle Pines, MN 55014-1796
   www.agsnet.com
   800-328-2560 or 651-287-7220

Comments
   The standardization established six-month norms from which the authors mathematically derived norms for three-month intervals. Given the uneven nature of child development, some might question this practice. In addition, the authors provide age equivalents—a practice that has been widely criticized.

The authors of the ESP are also authors of the assessments used in the concurrent validity studies. Some of the items on the ESP are derived from the longer assessments and share many common features (Telzrow 1995).

The sensitivity information available on the ESP indicates only moderate sensitivity levels. This means that a significant percentage of children who should be referred may not be identified using this instrument.

Supplementary Information

Barnett, D.W. 1995. Review of the AGS Early Screening Profiles. In *The twelfth mental measurements yearbook,* eds. J.C. Conoley & J.C. Impara, 61–63. Lincoln, NE: Buros Institute of Mental Measurements.

Nuttall, E.V., I. Romero, & J. Kalesnik, eds. 1999. *Assessing and screening preschoolers: Psychological and educational dimensions.* 2d ed. Needham Heights, MA: Allyn & Bacon.

Telzrow, C. 1995. Review of the AGS Early Screening Profiles. In *The twelfth mental measurements yearbook,* eds. J.C. Conoley & J.C. Impara, 63–65. Lincoln, NE: Buros Institute of Mental Measurements.

Denver II (1990)

Authors: W.F. Frankenburg, J. Dodds, P. Archer, B. Bresnick, P. Maschka, N. Edelmen, & H. Shapiro

Age ranges: 2 weeks to 6 years

The amount of **time** for administration is 20–25 minutes for entire test; 10–15 minutes for the abbreviated version.

The instrument is designed to be **administered** by teachers, specialists, or volunteers if properly trained.

The following **training materials** are available:
- Videotape
- Training proficiency program

The **developmental areas** covered by the test:
> The Denver II consists of more than 120 items from which a selection is made for a specific age range. The items are grouped in four areas: personal/social, fine motor/adaptive, language, and gross motor. In response to concerns raised about the Denver Developmental Screening Test (DDST), the Denver II added 14 items (primarily language items), omitted 18 items from the DDST, and changed 18 items. A brief behavior scale, on which examiners rate compliance, fearfulness, interest, and attention, has been added.

This instrument provides for **parent input** through: parent report items.

The **languages** available other than English: Spanish.

The following **statistical information** is available:
> *Standardized norms* were developed based on a nonrepresentative sample of 2,096 children. The sample was not stratified and the majority of the sample was from Colorado. There was an underrepresentation of Black children and an overrepresentation of children of White mothers with education levels greater than 12 years.

Reliability

Interobserver	= .99*
Test-retest	= .90

*Does not include ratings of behavior or speech intelligibility.

Validity

Concurrent	= N/A**
Predictive	= N/A**
Sensitivity***	= .55–.83 (Glascoe et al. 1992)
Specificity***	= .43–.80 (Glascoe et al. 1992)

**The authors assert that convergent validity studies would be meaningless because the instrument is not measuring a unitary construct. In addition, they say that current child development instrumentation is inadequate to support construct validity studies. The authors also note that the Denver II should not be used to make predictions about later need for special education services.

***The sensitivity and specificity information from Glascoe et al. (1992) represents two methods of scoring. One method yielded acceptable sensitivity (.83) with low specificity (.43), and the other yielded low sensitivity (.56) with acceptable specificity (.80).

The total **cost** of the test is $90/English version; $120/Spanish version.

Score sheets: $25 for 100 English-speaking children; $29 for 100 Spanish-speaking children.

The instrument is **available from:**
Denver Developmental Materials, Inc.
P.O. Box 371075
Denver, CO 80237-5075
www.denverii.com
800-419-4729 or 303-355-4729

Comments

The Denver II is the revised version of the Denver Developmental Screening Test (DDST). The DDST is one of the most widely used screening instruments available and has been used in more than 54 countries (Hughes 1995).

Like its predecessor, the Denver II is easy to administer and score. Concerns raised about the DDST regarding the need for additional language items, the need for increased test sensitivity, application of the norms to different ethnic groups, and questions about the applicability of some of the items prompted the authors to create the current revision in addition to renorming the test. On the Denver II only 31 percent of the items can be scored by report, compared with almost half of the DDST. However, there continue to be concerns about the Denver II, particularly in the areas of validity (Glascoe et al. 1992; Hughes 1995; Mirenda 1995).

The study by Glascoe and her colleagues (1992) indicated that there would still be a high rate of under-referrals or over-referrals depending upon the cutoff used. The authors did not conduct concurrent or predictive validity studies. Seventeen items on the Denver II had significantly different norms for one or more subgroups (Mirenda 1995). Data are provided in the technical manual to aide in interpretation of scores with children from diverse backgrounds (Mirenda 1995), but it is not likely that most users will consult the technical manual when interpreting scores. Until adequate validity and sensitivity/specificity have been demonstrated, caution is advised in interpreting the results.

The authors of the Denver II expressed concern about inappropriate administration of the instrument and misinterpretation of the results. They caution that the test be used only to give a brief overview of the child's development, reflecting the child's biological intactness and past experiences. It is not designed to yield a Developmental Quotient (the developmental age divided by the chronological age multiplied by 100, with a DQ less than 85 indicating a developmental delay), nor is it designed to predict later learning disabilities, emotional problems, or special education placements (Frankenburg et al. 1992, 96).

Supplementary Information

Frankenburg, W., J. Dodds, P. Archer, H. Shapiro, & B. Bresnick. 1992. The Denver II: A major revision and restandardization of the Denver Developmental Screening Test. *Pediatrics* 89 (1): 91–97.

Glascoe, F., K.E. Byrne, L.G. Ashford, K.L. Johnson, B. Chang, & B. Strickland. 1992. Accuracy of the Denver II in developmental screening. *Pediatrics* 89 (6, Pt. 2): 1221–25.

Hughes, S. 1995. Review of the Denver II. In *The twelfth mental measurements yearbook,* eds. J.C. Conoley & J.C. Impala, 263–64. Lincoln, NE: Buros Institute of Mental Measurements.

Mirenda, P. 1995. Review of the Denver II. In *The twelfth mental measurements yearbook,* eds. J.C. Conoley & J.C. Impala, 265–66. Lincoln, NE: Buros Institute of Mental Measurements.

Developmental Indicators for the Assessment of Learning-3rd Ed. (DIAL-3; 1998); Speed DIAL (short-form version)

Authors: C. Mardell-Czudnowski & D.S. Goldenberg

Age ranges: 3 years to 6 years, 11 months

The amount of **time** for administration is 20–30 minutes. (Speed DIAL is 15–20 minutes.)

The instrument is designed to be **administered** by a professional coordinator and trained screeners.

The following **training materials** are available:
- Handbooks
- Manual
- Training workshop with written tests, performance tests, and scripts for role play
- Videotape

The **developmental areas** covered by the test:
The full DIAL-3 includes motor (direct observation), concepts (direct observation), language (direct observation), self-help development (parent report), and social development (parent report). The language section includes items that require the child to name letters and produce sounds for letters, produce a rhyme for a stimulus word, and produce a word that has the same initial sound as a target word. Articulation, problem solving, naming objects and actions, and providing personal information are also included on the language portion of the DIAL-3. The Speed DIAL has only 10 items and provides a total score only.

This instrument provides for **parent input** through: parent questionnaires of self-help and social development, medical history, family background, and general concerns. Parent form is scored separately.

The **languages** available other than English: Spanish*.

> * The manual states that the DIAL-3 was "normed on a national sample of Spanish-speaking children" (Mardell-Czudnowski & Goldenberg 1998, 3). However, the authors relied on a procedure called "equating" to develop the norms, a method that Cizek (2001) labeled "suspect."

The following **statistical information** is available:

> *Standardized norms* developed on a nationally representative sample of 1,560 English-speaking children. A separate sample of 605 Spanish-speaking children was used for the Spanish version.

Reliability

Interobserver	= N/A
Test-retest	= Total score .84–.88 (motor area reliabilities are weakest at .67–.69)

Validity

Concurrent*	= .55 (*Battelle Developmental Inventory*)
(Screening Test)	= .38–.61 (total DIAL-3 with *Early Screening Profiles*)
	= .53 (*Brigance Preschool Screen*)
	= .52–.79 (*Differential Ability Scales* General Conceptual Composite. Highest correlation is the DIAL-3 total with the *DAS* General Conceptual Composite; similar subtest score correlations are low to moderate)
	= .57–.69 (DIAL-3 Language with the *Peabody Picture Vocabulary Test-III*)
	= .03–.72 (*Social Skills Rating System*. Highest correlation is with the parent version of the *SSRS*. Relationships with teacher versions were all below .21 uncorrected and below .33 corrected)

*All coefficients were corrected for limited variability.

Predictive	= N/A
Sensitivity	= .83 (total score with *Differential Ability Scales*) (.53 for motor; .57 for cognition)

| Specificity | = .86 (total score with *Differential Ability Scales*) (.96 for motor; 1.0 for cognition) |

The total **cost** of the test is $449.99 ($548.99 with the computer scoring program).

Speed DIAL kit: $169.99.

Score sheets: $61.99 for 50 children (record forms, cutting cards, parent questionnaires).

The instrument is **available from:**

AGS Publishing
4201 Woodland Road
Circle Pines, MN 55014-1796
www.agsnet.com
800-328-2560 or 651-287-7220

Comments

The DIAL-3 "appears to be a stronger and better standardized screening instrument than the earlier editions" (Fairbank 2001) while retaining the features that made the earlier versions attractive to users (Cizek 2001).

According to the recommended administration, each section of the DIAL-3 is administered by a different adult, requiring the child to transition from one task to another every 10 minutes. Each adult reports on the child's behavior and attention for her or his section of the test. The Speed DIAL is administered by a single individual. The administration instructions and materials are easy to use (Cizek 2001). The manual includes information about how to conduct every step of the screening (from the planning to sharing the results with parents).

Item Response Theory (Rasch) was used to identify mis-fitting items from previous versions and to aid in development of this version.

The DIAL-3 and Speed DIAL have moderate sensitivity for communication disabilities. The mean scores for children with identified disabilities in communication were 86.7 on the DIAL-3, 84.7 on the language subtest of the DIAL-3, 88.3 on the cognitive subtest, and 87.5 on the Speed DIAL. Communication disabilities were the largest group of children in the sample of children with special needs (137/161). The authors conjecture that these children may have had articulation problems.

Supplementary Information

Cizek, G.J. 2001. Review of the Developmental Indicators for the Assessment of Learning, 3rd ed. In *The fourteenth mental measurements yearbook*, eds. B.S. Plake & J.C. Impara, 394–98. Lincoln, NE: Buros Institute of Mental Measurements.

Fairbank, D.W. 2001. Review of the Developmental Indicators for the Assessment of Learning, 3rd ed. In *The fourteenth mental measurements yearbook*, eds. B.S. Plake & J.C. Impara, 398–400. Lincoln, NE: Buros Institute of Mental Measurements.

Mardell-Czudnowski, C., & D.S. Goldenberg. 2000. A new test for assessing preschool motor development: DIAL-3. *Adapted Physical Activity Quarterly* 17: 78–94.

Early Screening Inventory·Revised (ESI·R; 1997)

Authors: S.J. Meisels, D.B. Marsden, M.S. Wiske, & L.W. Henderson

Age ranges: 3 years to 6 years (two forms: one used for ages 3 years to 4½ years called the ESI-P; and one for ages 4½ years to 6 years called the ESI-K)

The amount of **time** for administration is 15–20 minutes.

The instrument is designed to be **administered** by teachers, specialists, or trained paraprofessionals or volunteers. Knowledge of child development and training is recommended. Information about an online version is available at www.esiscreen.com.

The following **training materials** are available:
- Videotapes
- Training kit with trainer's manual, reproducible masters, and two videos

The **developmental areas** covered by the test:
The ESI-R samples visual-motor/adaptive, language and cognition, and gross motor performance. Referral decisions are made on the overall performance of the child. Cutoff scores provided by six-month age intervals classify children's performance into Refer, Rescreen, or OK.

This instrument provides for **parent input** through: parent questionnaire.

The **languages** available other than English: Spanish.

The following **statistical information** is available:
Standardized norms were developed separately for the two English forms (ESI-P and ESI-K) and are described that way below:

ESI-P
The standardized norms were developed with a sample of 977 children drawn from 16 preschools or child care programs in five states. Approximately half the sample was male (52 percent), 53 percent of the children were White (non-Hispanic), 21

percent were African American, and 26 percent were Asian American, American Indian, or other groups. Approximately 30 percent of the mothers and fathers had not completed high school. Nearly 87 percent of the children attended Head Start programs.

Reliability

Interobserver	= .99 (based on 35 tester-observer pairs)
Test-retest	= .98 (7–10 days apart; two different examiners)

Validity

Concurrent	= N/A
Predictive	= .73 (4–6 months later with *McCarthy Scales of Children's Abilities*)
Sensitivity	= .92
Specificity	= .80

ESI-K

The sample for the ESI-K includes data collected on 5,034 children enrolled in 60 classrooms in 10 states with roughly equal numbers of males and females. Seventy percent of the children were White (non-Hispanic), 16 percent were African American, 20 percent had mothers with less than a high school education, and 32 percent were enrolled in Head Start.

Reliability

Interobserver	= .97 (based on 586 tester-observer pairs)
Test-retest	= .87 (7–10 days apart; two different examiners)

Validity

Concurrent	= N/A
Predictive	= .73 (7–9 months later with *McCarthy Scales of Children's Abilities*)
Sensitivity	= .93
Specificity	= .80

The total **cost** of the test is $115.95 for each version.
Score sheets: $29.95 for 30 children.

The instrument is **available from:**

Pearson Early Learning
1185 Avenue of the Americas
New York, NY 11030

Customer Service
145 S. Mt. Zion Road
P.O. Box 2500
Lebanon, IN 46052
www.PearsonEarlyLearning.com
800-321-3106

Comments

The ESI·R is easy to administer, and training materials are available. The manual assists users in every aspect of the screening process. It is a research-based instrument (McWayne, Fantuzzo, & McDermott 2004; Meisels, Henderson, Liaw, Browning, & Ten Have 1993). Online scoring is available.

The parent questionnaire is used to provide supplementary information and is not intended for making independent screening decisions.

The ESI·R was very carefully constructed. Earlier versions of the ESI·R demonstrated predictive validity with performance in kindergarten and the primary grades (Kimmel 2001). The ESI·R represents one of the most accurate and stable preschool screening instruments available today, and has been described as setting "the gold standard" for developmental screening (Paget 2001, 452).

Supplementary Information

Kimmel, E. 2001. Review of the Early Screening Inventory·Revised. In *The fourteenth mental measurements yearbook,* eds. B.S. Plake & J.C. Impara, 451–52. Lincoln, NE: Buros Institute of Mental Measurements.

McWayne, C.M., J.W. Fantuzzo, & P.A. McDermott. 2004. Preschool competency in context: An investigation of the unique contribution of child competencies to early academic success. *Developmental Psychology* 40 (4): 633–45.

Meisels, S.J., L.W. Henderson, F. Liaw, K. Browning, & T. Ten Have. 1993. New evidence for the effectiveness of the Early Screening Inventory. *Early Childhood Research Quarterly* 8: 327–46.

Paget, K.D. 2001. Review of the Early Screening Inventory-Revised. In *The fourteenth mental measurements yearbook,* eds. B.S. Plake & J.C. Impara, 452–53. Lincoln, NE: Buros Institute of Mental Measurements.

First Screening Test for Evaluating Preschoolers (FirstSTEp; 1993)

Author: L.J. Miller

Age ranges: 2.9 years to 6.2 years

The amount of **time** for administration is 15 minutes. If the Adaptive Behavior Checklist is completed by parent interview by the examiner, the total time of administration would be 25–30 minutes.

The instrument is designed to be **administered** individually by teachers, specialists, and properly trained volunteers. Administrators should be familiar with child development and be trained in the administration of the instrument. The manual also discusses administration to several children at a time utilizing multiple examiners.

The following **training materials** are available:
- Detailed instructions in the manual
- Videotapes

The **developmental areas** covered by the test:
Twelve subtests are grouped for scoring into cognitive, communication, and motor. There is an optional social-emotional scale and adaptive behavior checklist. Separate forms are available for ages 2.9–3.8 years, 3.9–4.8 years, and 4.9–6.2 years. The 12 subtests are presented to the children as games.

This instrument provides for **parent input** through: The adaptive behavior checklist assesses daily living skills, self-management, functioning within a community, and social interaction. It is optional, and recommended administration is parent interview. The parent/teacher scale is designed to assess behavior and is completed by an adult who knows the child well. Areas addressed on the social-emotional rating scale and parent/teacher rating checklist are attention/activity levels, social interactions, personality traits, and behavior problems.

The **languages** available other than English: Spanish.

The following **statistical information** is available:
Standardized norms are available by age and sex.

Reliability*

Interobserver = .91 (with trained examiners)

Test-retest = .90

*Reliability estimates are for the domains.

Validity

Concurrent = .82 (with WPPSI)

= .64 (motor domain with *Bruininks-Oseretsky Test of Motor Proficiency)*

= .61–.76 (language domain, with the *Test of Language Development, 2nd Ed.)*

= .29–.56 (composite score with the subscales of the *Vineland Scales of Adaptive Behavior)*

= .65 (parent/teacher scale with the *Walker Problem Behavior Identification Checklist-Revised)*

Predictive = N/A

Sensitivity** = .72 (language domain) to .85 (cognitive domain)

Specificity = .76 (language domain subsample A) to .83 (language domain subsample B)

**Sensitivity and specificity are based on subsamples each composed of children from the standardization sample and from the clinical validity sample.

The total **cost** of the test is $225.

Score sheets: $40 for 25 children for record forms; and $40 for 25 social-emotional/adaptive behavior checklists; and $22 for 25 parent/teacher rating checklists.

The instrument is **available from:**

The Psychological Corporation
Harcourt Assessment, Inc.
19500 Bulverde Road
San Antonio, TX 78259-3701
http://harcourtassessment.com
800-211-8378

Comments

FirstSTEp was very carefully constructed. In addition to cognitive, communication, and social-emotional development, this instrument addresses neurodevelopmental and sensoryintegration abilities of young children.

The manual includes detailed information about test administration, and two videos are available to assist in training. The examiners in the validity and reliability studies received three days of training.

Social and Emotional Screening Instruments

The parents of nearly 5 percent of children 4 to 7 years old report that their children have *"definite or severe difficulties* with emotions, concentration, behavior, or being able to get along with other people" (Federal Interagency Forum on Child and Family Statistics 2005). These difficulties can persist and cause lifelong problems (U.S. Department of Health and Human Services 1999). Early identification and intervention is important. As noted in this guide, it is more difficult to screen for early social and emotional difficulties than for cognitive, language, and motor problems, but several measures have recently been developed to address this need. The instruments reviewed in this appendix are designed to identify social and emotional difficulties in preschool children.

In addition to the instruments reviewed here, a number of instruments have been developed to identify children who have early signs of autism or pervasive developmental disorders. Autism is a disorder of social-emotional and communication development that affects 1 in 500 children (Filipek et al. 2000). Identification should occur between birth and age 3 so intensive intervention can be started as early as possible. Children with autism show measurable "problems with eye contact, orienting to one's name, joint attention, pretend play, imitation, nonverbal communication and language development" by 18 months of age (Filipek et al. 2000, 471). Specific instruments have been designed to screen for autism (e.g., *Checklist for Autism in Toddlers;* for children older than 4 years, the *Autism Screening Questionnaire).* Additional diagnostic instruments are being developed to help differentiate pervasive developmental disorder from other developmental and language delays.

Contents:

- Ages and Stages Questionnaires: Social Emotional (ASQ:SE)
- Devereux Early Childhood Assessment (DECA)
- Early Screening Project (ESP)
- Preschool and Kindergarten Behavior Scales-2nd Ed. (PKBS-2)
- Temperament and Atypical Behavior Scales (TABS); Temperament and Atypical Behavior Scales Screener (TABS Screener)

Ages and Stages Questionnaires: Social Emotional (ASQ:SE; 2002)

Authors: J. Squires, D. Bricker, & E. Twombly

Age ranges: 3 months to 66 months

The amount of **time** for administration is 10–20 minutes.

The instrument is designed to be **administered** by parents completing and partially scoring independently; a professional completes the scoring and provides interpretation.

The following **training materials** are available:
- Detailed instructions
- Videotape

The **areas** covered by the test:
The ASQ:SE addresses self-regulation, compliance with adults, communication, adaptive behaviors, affect, autonomy, and social interaction. The test addresses both social-emotional competence and the presence or absence of problem behaviors. The number of items ranges from 21 (6-month form) to 32 (24- to 60-month forms).

This instrument provides for **parent input** through: parent completion of the questionnaire.

The **languages** available other than English: Spanish.

The following **statistical information** is available:
Standardized norms with more than 3,000 children.

Reliability

Interobserver	= N/A
Test-retest	= 94% agreement

Validity

Concurrent	= .81–.95 (with the *Child Behavior Checklist* and *Social-Emotional Early Childhood Scales*)
Predictive	= N/A

Sensitivity   = .82 (range = .75 [24 months] to .89
                  [36 months])
Specificity   = .92 (range = .88 [30 months] to .95
                  [6 months])

The total **cost** of the test is $125.
   Score sheets: Forms can be photocopied.

The instrument is **available from:**
   Brookes Publishing Co.
   P.O. Box 10624
   Baltimore, MD 21285-0624
   www.brookespublishing.com
   800-638-3775

Comments

Complements the general developmental monitoring ASQ. Separate questionnaires for 6, 12, 24, 30, 36, 48, and 60 months. Internal consistency is adequate overall (.82), but was lower for the 6- and 12-month questionnaires (coefficient alpha=.69 and .67 respectively) (Squires, Bricker, Heo, & Twombly 2001).

The authors administered a measure of the social validity of the ASQ:SE to a sample of 731 parents. Parents indicated that the questionnaires were easy to understand, appropriate for their child, and helped the parent to think about the social and emotional development of their child (Squires, Bricker, Heo, & Twombly 2001).

In addition to being asked to report on the frequency with which a child exhibits a behavior, parents are also asked to check any item that is a concern.

Supplementary Information

Squires, J., D. Bricker, K. Heo, & E. Twombly. 2001. Identification of social-emotional problems in young children using a parent-completed screening measure. *Early Childhood Research Quarterly* 16: 405–19.

Devereux Early Childhood Assessment (DECA; 1999); Devereux Early Childhood Assessment—Clinical Edition (DECA-C; 2004)

Authors: P.A. LeBuffe & J.A. Naglieri

Age ranges: 2 years to 5 years

The amount of **time** for administration is 10 minutes.

The instrument is designed to be **administered** based on classroom observations or parent ratings. Respondent needs to have contact with the child at least two hours at a time for a minimum of two days a week for four weeks.

The following **training materials** are available:
- Parent guides
- Training sessions

The **areas** covered by the test:
> The DECA has the following scales: initiative, self-control, attachment, total protective factors (37 positive items), behavioral concerns (10 items). The DECA-C has 62 items that examine the positive behaviors and then more closely examine attention problems, aggression, withdrawal/depression, and emotional control problems.

This instrument provides for **parent input** through: parent completion of the forms.

The **languages** available other than English: Spanish.

The following **statistical information** is available:
> *Standardized norms* with two nationally representative samples (N=2,000 and N=1,108). No age difference found.

Reliability

Interobserver	= .57–.77 (teacher to teacher); parent to teacher and parent to parent ranged from .19 to .44
Test-retest	= .87–.91 positive scales—teachers
	= .57–.80 positive scales—parents
	= .68 behavioral concerns—teachers
	= .55 behavioral concerns—parents

Validity

Concurrent	= N/A
Predictive	= N/A
Sensitivity	= .67–.78
Specificity	= .65–.71

The total **cost** of the test is $199.95 per kit (with 40 forms) (DECA); $125.95 (DECA-C).

Score sheets: $39.95 for 40 children (DECA; guides and observation journals are an additional cost); $59.95 for 30 children (DECA-C); E-DECA (Web-based computer version of the DECA) annual fee $249.95.

The instrument is **available from:**

Kaplan Early Learning Company
1310 Lewisville-Clemmons Road
Lewisville, NC 27023-9635
www.kaplanco.com
800-334-2014

Comments

The DECA was developed based on review of the literature on resiliency and child specific protective factors. A developmental model was not used, and age differences were not found in the normative sample. A strong link is provided between the assessment and the curriculum that accompanies it. The items are clearly written and require only a sixth grade reading level. The DECA identifies individual child strengths and can be used in planning. It is not recommended for use in eligibility decisions, and caution is advised in using the parent ratings (Chittooran 2003).

Evidence on the clinical version was not available at the time of this review. It will be important to examine its validity.

Observation summary form is available, and an infant-toddler version is under development.

Supplementary Information

Buhs, E.S. 2003. Review of the Devereux Early Childhood Assessment. In *The fifteenth mental measurements yearbook,* eds. B.S. Plake, J.C. Impara, & R.A. Spies, 314–16. Lincoln, NE: Buros Institute of Mental Measurements.

Chittooran, M.R.M. 2003. Review of the Devereux Early Childhood Assessment. In *The fifteenth mental measurements yearbook,* eds. B.S. Plake, J.C. Impara, & R.A. Spies, 312–14. Lincoln, NE: Buros Institute of Mental Measurements.

Early Screening Project (ESP; 1995)

Authors: H.M. Walker, H.H. Severson, & E.G. Feil

Age ranges: 3 years to 6 years

The amount of **time** for administration is 60 minutes (total group).

The instrument is designed to be **administered** using a multistage approach:

Stage 1: Ranking all children and rating the top three to five in each behavioral area

Stage 2: Ratings of the five to six highest ranked children

Stage 3: Parent questionnaire and direct observation of children who exceeded the criteria in Stage 2.

The following **training materials** are available:
- Manual and protocols with definitions and examples
- Videotape for the observation procedures

The **areas** covered by the test:

The items rated in Stage 2 utilize a five-point frequency scale, except for the critical events items. The scales on the teacher ratings are social interaction (eight items), adaptive behavior scales (eight items), maladaptive behaviors (nine items), aggressive behaviors (nine items), and critical events (16 occurrence/non-occurrence items). The externalizing behaviors include both inappropriate behaviors and behavioral excesses (that are directed outwardly). Internalizing behaviors, such as problems with self-esteem or social avoidance, are also examined.

The parent questionnaires examine how the child plays with other children, how the child interacts with caregivers, how the child interacts with materials, and self-care.

The observations assess the social adjustment and interactions of children who were identified as being at risk on the Stage 2 ratings.

This instrument provides for **parent input** through: parent questionnaires and permission for observations.

The **languages** available other than English: [unknown].

The following **statistical information** is available:
Standardized norms with a large sample (N=2,853) drawn from eight states (not nationally representative). Separate norms are provided for males and females. More than one-third of the sample is from southeastern states. Low-income and rural children appear to be overrepresented (Grill 2001).

Reliability

Interobserver	= .42–.70 on the rankings, .48–.79 on the Stage 2 scales scores; .87–.88 on observations
Test-retest	= .59 (externalizing), .25 (internalizing), .75–.91 for the critical events and adaptive and maladaptive behaviors (six months)

Validity

Concurrent	= .19–.95 with the Behar and Conners rating scales (median correlations .69 with the Behar and .80 with the Conners rating scale)
Predictive	= see comments below
Sensitivity	= *62%–100% true positives
Specificity	= *94%–100% true negatives

*Discriminant function was used with teacher recommendations of behaviorally disordered, rather than with clinically identified children. In addition, the size and characteristics of the sample were not described.

The total **cost** of the test is $100.95 (includes manual, reproducibles, stopwatch, and training video).

The instrument is **available from:**
Sopris West
4093 Specialty Place
Longmont, CO 80504-5400
www.sopriswest.com
800-547-6747 or 303-651-2829

Comments

ESP is an extension of the *Systematic Screening for Behavior Disorders (SSBD;* Walker & Severson 1990). It is intended to be a proactive screening to support childfind efforts and prevent the long-term negative outcomes associated with poor social and emotional skills.

Definitions, criteria, and standards are provided to increase reliability in ranking and rating students. No significant differences were found by ethnicity.

ESP predicted special education eligibility, grade retention, behavioral, referral, and other negative comments on behavior four years later (third grade). Moderate correlations were found between the ESP and measures of social-emotional functioning (also four years later). The strongest relationship was found between the prosocial behavior ratings (adaptive rating scale).

Knoff (2001) cautions that the potential exists to misinterpret behavior and to "prematurely categorize or label children with these behaviors." Knoff acknowledges that the authors address these concerns in the manual, but adds concerns about the level of professional who interprets the ESP results.

The authors of the ESP along with other colleagues developed an intervention program to help preschool and primary age children develop necessary social skills.

Supplementary Information

Grill, J.J. 2001. Review of the Early Screening Project. In *The fourteenth mental measurements yearbook,* eds. B.S. Plake & J. C. Impara, 453–54. Lincoln, NE: Buros Institute of Mental Measurements.

Knoff, H.M. 2001. Review of the Early Screening Project. In *The fourteenth mental measurements yearbook,* eds. B.S. Plake & J.C. Impara, 455–57. Lincoln, NE: Buros Institute of Mental Measurements.

Printz, P.H., A. Borg, & M.A. Demaree. 2003. *A look at social, emotional, and behavioral screening tools for Head Start and Early Head Start.* Boston, MA: Education Development Center, Inc. Online: http://notes.edc.org/CCF/ccflibrary.nsf/Libauthors?OpenView.

Walker, H.M., & H.H. Severson. 1990. *Systematic screening for behavior disorders.* Longmont, CO: Sopris West.

Walker, H.M., B. Stiller, A. Golly, K. Kavanagh, H.H. Severson, & E.G. Feil. 1997. *First steps to success: preschool edition.* Longmont, CO: Sopris West.

Preschool and Kindergarten Behavior Scales-2nd Ed. (PKBS-2; 2002)

Author: K.W. Merrell

Age ranges: 3 years to 6 years

The amount of **time** for administration is 8–12 minutes.

The test can be **administered** through teacher ratings and/or parent ratings. Both home and school norms are available.

The following **training materials** are available:
• Manual

The **areas** covered by the test:
Both positive behaviors (34 items) and problem behaviors (42 items) are examined. The resultant scales are social interaction, social independence, social cooperation, total social skills, externalizing problems, internalizing problems, and problem behavior total. There are additional optional supplemental subscales: self-centered/explosive, attention problems/overactive, antisocial/aggressive, social withdrawal, and anxiety/somatic problems.

This instrument provides for **parent input** through: parent completion of the ratings.

The **languages** available other than English: Spanish.

The following **statistical information** is available:
Standardized norms developed for the original PKBS (1995) with a large sample (N=2,855) that was supplemented with 458 additional cases for the PKBS-2. The sample is racially and ethnically representative of the U.S. census population, but 77 percent of the sample was from the West, and 3-year-olds are relatively underrepresented (Madle 2005).

Reliability

Interobserver	= .36–.63 (teachers and aides); .13–.57 (home and school raters)
Test-retest	= .58–.87 (three weeks)

Validity

Concurrent = moderate to strong correlations across multiple studies with seven different assessments*

Predictive = N/A

* Using a discriminant function with children with developmental disabilities and typically developing children, 71 percent of the children were correctly classified. Significant differences were found between the scores of typically developing children and children with attention deficit hyperactivity disorder (ADHD), and children nominated by teachers as having internalizing or externalizing problem behaviors.

The total **cost** of the test is $110.
Score sheets: $41 for 50 children.

The instrument is **available from:**
PRO-ED, Inc.
8700 Shoal Creek Blvd.
Austin, TX 78757-6897
www.proedinc.com
800-897-3202

Comments

The development of this instrument was based on the research on preschool typical and atypical behavior. It was developed as an assessment for preschools and kindergartens. Given its brevity, it is sometimes recommended for screening purposes (Niemeyer & Scott-Little 2001; Printz, Borg, & Demaree 2003), though sensitivity and specificity have not been researched. The manual includes multiple uses for the PKBS-2 including a screening tool and a multiple setting assessment for use in identifying children in need of intervention.

The authors reported that differences by age and gender were relatively small, and so separate norms tables are provided only for settings. However, the 3-year-old sample size was small (N=147), and raw score changes from 3 to 4 years old are more than one-third of a standard deviation. This could lead to an overidentification of 3-year-olds. Madle (2005) cautions against its use with 3-year-olds.

Supplementary Information

Fairbank, D.W. 2005. Review of the Preschool and Kindergarten Behavior Scales-Second Edition. In *The sixteenth mental measurements yearbook,* eds. R.A. Spies & B.S. Plake. Lincoln, NE: Buros Institute of Mental Measurements.

Madle, R.A. 2005. Review of the Preschool and Kindergarten Behavior Scales-Second Edition. In *The sixteenth mental measurements yearbook,* eds. R.A. Spies & B.S. Plake. Lincoln, NE: Buros Institute of Mental Measurements.

Niemeyer, J., & C. Scott-Little. 2001. Assessing kindergarten children: A compendium of assessment instruments. Tallahassee, FL: SERVE. Online: www.serve.org/_downloads/publications/rdakcc.pdf.

Printz, P.H., A. Borg, & M.A. Demaree. 2003. *A look at social, emotional and behavioral screening tools for Head Start and Early Head Start.* Boston, MA: Center for Children and Families Education Development Center, Inc. Online: http://notes.edc.org/CCF/ccflibrary.nsf/Libauthors?OpenView.

Temperament and Atypical Behavior Scales (TABS; 1999); Temperament and Atypical Behavior Scales Screener (TABS Screener; 1999)

Authors: S.J. Bagnato, J.T. Neisworth, J. Salvia, & F.M. Hunt

Age ranges: 11 months to 71 months

The amount of **time** for administration is 5 minutes for the Screener; 15 minutes for full TABS.

The instrument is designed to be **administered** by parent interview or independently completed by parent with explanation by professional. Professional interpretation is recommended.

The following **training materials** are available:
 • Instructions in manual

The **areas** covered by the test:
  TABS addresses typical and atypical self-regulation. The TABS Screener asks about the presence or absence of 15 self-regulation problems.

This instrument provides for **parent input** through: parent report.

The **languages** available other than English: none.

The following **statistical information** is available:
  Standardized norms developed on a sample of almost 1,000 children from diverse socioeconomic and ethnic backgrounds. Detailed information on the normative sample for the Screener was not available in the TABS assessment manual.

Reliability
  Interobserver/cross environment
             = .64 (TABS); subtests .42–.62
  Test-retest   = .81–.94

Validity
  Concurrent   = 83% classification
               agreement with TABS

Predictive   = N/A
Sensitivity   = *
Specificity   = *

*Sensitivity and specificity are reported only in relationship of the TABS Screener to the full TABS.

The total **cost** of the test is $85.
    Screening protocols: $25 for 50 children.
    Assessment forms: $30 for 30 children.

The instrument is **available from:**
    Brookes Publishing Co.
    P.O. Box 10624
    Baltimore, MD 21285-0624
    www.brookespublishing.com
    800-638-3775

Comments
    The Screener has 15 items.
    Without detailed information about the normative sample, it is difficult to know how accurate this assessment will be for diverse samples. More information about the validity of the instrument is needed, especially studies of the sensitivity and specificity of the Screener for identifying children with disabilities.

Reliability and Validity

Reliability

Several types of reliability are reported for screening instruments.

In the *interobserver* (or scorer reliability) procedure, an examiner and observer each score the same performance of the child on the test, rendering two sets of scores for that administration of the test. A statistical value called the "reliability coefficient" is calculated from the percentage of agreement between the two people scoring the same test performance. Reliability coefficients for developmental assessments should be greater than .80. Higher coefficients indicate more reliable scores.

In the *test-retest* (or test stability) procedure, two different examiners administer the screening instrument to the same child within approximately one week. The reliability score obtained in this fashion describes the stability of the instrument over time—that is, how consistent the results obtained at the two different time points are—as well as the percentage of agreement in results when the same child is screened by two different examiners. Sometimes test-retest reliability is based on two administrations to the same child by a single examiner at two points in time (approximately one week apart) and is then purely a measure of test stability. Stable, reliable assessments report test-retest reliabilities greater than .80, with higher coefficients indicating greater reliability. The time between administrations can affect the stability of the assessment. Because development in early childhood is rapid (in contrast to academic development in adolescents), if the time period between administrations is more than a week or two, the test-retest reliability may not be as high.

Finally, *internal* reliability data are also often reported, using such statistics as kappas or alphas. This is strictly a measure of a test's internal consistency and tells us only about the degree of similarity of an assessment's items. Items in a scale should have good internal consistency (greater than .80). Scales that are longer (that is, have more items) will generally report higher internal consistency coefficients.

Validity

Screening instruments often report both concurrent and predictive validity.

Most *concurrent* validity procedures compare screening results with outcomes derived from diagnostic assessments. The diagnostic assessment instrument must be reliable and valid, and should be administered shortly after the screening test (usually a week to 10 days). Validity would then be reported in terms of the agreement between the two tests.

In contrast, *predictive* validity scores are obtained when screening results are compared with measures of children's performance obtained several months later. These measures may take the form of diagnostic assessments, school achievement test scores, ratings by observers, or teacher reports. The shorter the length of time between the administrations, the stronger the correlation score should be.

Some screening tests present results in terms of *face* (or content) validity, that is, the independent judgment of professionals concerning the relevance of the items of a screening instrument. Face validity does not imply the administration of any assessments of a child or the completion of empirical research, where data is collected based on observation or experiments. Instead, face validity is imprecise, and should not be used as a substitute for other aspects of validity.

Most validity studies use correlational techniques to indicate the relationship between screening and outcomes. Unfortunately, correlations only describe the degree of overlap between two tests or measures. They imply that scores within a certain range on two different measures are associated with each other. They yield no information about the accuracy of a screening test's results, or the number of children who were over- or under-referred. To obtain that information one must compute the sensitivity and specificity of a test. The *sensitivity* of a test refers to the proportion of children at risk for developmental delay or significant problems in school who are correctly identified by the test. The *specificity* of a test refers to the proportion of children not at risk who are not labeled at-risk by the screening. These two proportions are the primary means of evaluating a screening test's capacity to correctly classify children as at-risk or not at-risk. No other indicator of validity provides this kind of information concerning the accuracy of specific predictions.

The figure on the next page graphically represents screening test validity and shows how to compute sensitivity and specificity. All children who are identified by the screening instrument as possibly having learning problems, and whose status is confirmed by follow-up assessment, would be included in *quadrant a.* Those children who are erroneously referred for assessment—the over-referrals—are included in *quadrant b.* Those children who are identified as at-risk on the diagnostic assessment, but who are missed by the screening test—the under-referrals—are included in *quadrant c.* The largest proportion of children screened is represented in *quadrant d.* These are the children who were not identified as at-risk on either the screening or follow-up. The formulas for computing sensitivity and specificity are derived from this matrix.

By virtue of their brevity and generality, screening instruments are never 100 percent accurate. All test developers must balance *b*, the measure of over-referrals, against *c*, the indicator of under-referrals. By adjusting the cutoff point between *OK* and *refer*, a test's over- or under-referral rate will be altered. In most cases, it is preferable to err on the side of over-referral for further assessment than to miss children who require intervention.

		Follow-up assessment	
		Intervention needs +	No intervention needs −
Screening test	At-risk: Refer for evaluation +	True positives a	False positives (over-referrals) b
	Not at-risk: Do not refer for evaluation −	False negatives (under-referrals) c	True negatives d

Sensitivity: The proportion of children at-risk who are correctly identified.

$$\frac{a}{a + c}$$

Specificity: The proportion of children not at-risk who are correctly excluded from further assessment.

$$\frac{d}{b + d}$$

Sample Parent Questionnaire

ESI·R™

Early Screening Inventory·Revised™ Meisels et al.
Parent Questionnaire

Date _____

CHILD INFORMATION

NAME _____ ☐ Male ☐ Female

HOME ADDRESS Street _____ Apt _____

City _____ State _____ Zip _____

Phone (_____) _____ Date of Birth _____

Who is completing this Parent Questionnaire?
☐ Mother ☐ Father ☐ Other Relative (specify) _____
☐ Guardian ☐ Caregiver ☐ Other (specify) _____

FAMILY

Mother

NAME _____

HOME ADDRESS Street _____ Apt _____

☐ same as child's   City _____ State _____ Zip _____

Phone (_____) _____ Date of Birth _____

EDUCATION Highest Grade Completed _____

OCCUPATION (be specific) _____

Father

NAME _____

HOME ADDRESS Street _____ Apt _____

☐ same as child's   City _____ State _____ Zip _____

Phone (_____) _____ Date of Birth _____

EDUCATION Highest Grade Completed _____

OCCUPATION (be specific) _____

Other Family Information

With whom has the child lived for most of the past year?
☐ Mother ☐ Father ☐ Both ☐ Guardian
☐ Other (specify) _____

Other children in the family –How many older? _____ How many younger? _____

Other people living in the household _____

What language(s) are spoken at home? ☐ English ☐ Other (specify) _____

PRESCHOOL/CHILD CARE HISTORY

Has your child attended preschool/child care before? ☐ Yes ☐ No

If yes, for how long? ☐ 6 months ☐ 1 year ☐ 2 years ☐ more than 2 years

Name of child's present or most recent school _____

ISBN 1-57212-083-5   © 2003 Pearson Education, Inc., publishing as Pearson Early Learning, New York, NY 10036. All rights reserved.
Early Screening Inventory-Revised, ESI-R, and the ESI-R logo are trademarks of Pearson Education, Inc.

1

MEDICAL HISTORY

Birth

Were there any significant problems during pregnancy? ☐ Yes ☐ No

If yes, please explain:

_____

_____

_____

Was your child more than 3 weeks premature? ☐ Yes ☐ No

If yes, how many weeks premature? _____

Baby's birth weight _____

Did the baby stay in the hospital longer than the mother? ☐ Yes ☐ No

If yes, please explain:

_____

_____

_____

At the time of birth, did the baby —   have seizures? ☐ Yes ☐ No

   turn blue? ☐ Yes ☐ No

Child's Health Since Birth

EYES

Has your child ever had trouble seeing? ☐ Yes ☐ No

Does your child hold books and objects close to his or her face? ☐ Yes ☐ No

Have your child's eyes ever looked crossed? ☐ Yes ☐ No

Have you ever suspected that your child has vision problems? ☐ Yes ☐ No

If yes, please explain:

_____

_____

_____

EARS

Has your child had frequent ear infections? ☐ Yes ☐ No

Has your child ever had trouble hearing? ☐ Yes ☐ No

Have you ever suspected that your child has hearing problems? ☐ Yes ☐ No

If yes, please explain:

_____

_____

_____

COORDINATION

Has your child ever had trouble walking, climbing, reaching, holding on to things? ☐ Yes ☐ No

If yes, please explain:

_____

_____

_____

2

**Child's Health
Since Birth** continued

Has your child ever had any significant injuries or hospitalizations? ☐ Yes ☐ No
If yes, please explain:

_____

_____

_____

Does your child have allergies? ☐ Yes ☐ No
If yes, please describe:

_____

_____

_____

Is your child presently on any medications? ☐ Yes ☐ No
If yes, please describe:

_____

_____

_____

Please describe any other health concerns:

_____

_____

_____

_____

_____

_____

CHILD'S DEVELOPMENT

Can your child —

feed him or herself using a spoon and/or a fork?	☐ Yes ☐ No
wash and dry his or her own hands?	☐ Yes ☐ No
help with dressing or dress with little assistance?	☐ Yes ☐ No
stay with a babysitter?	☐ Yes ☐ No
speak so that he or she can be understood by others?	☐ Yes ☐ No
express his or her thoughts and needs easily?	☐ Yes ☐ No

Do you have any concerns about your child's appetite or willingness to try ☐ Yes ☐ No
different foods?
If yes, please explain:

_____

_____

_____

3

Do you have any concerns about your child's sleeping patterns (going to bed with difficulty or waking often during the night)?   ☐ Yes ☐ No

If yes, please explain:

_____

_____

_____

| Is your child — | highly active? | ☐ Yes ☐ No |
| | very quiet? | ☐ Yes ☐ No |

| Is your child — | toilet trained during the day? | ☐ Yes ☐ No |
| | in need of help with toileting? | ☐ Yes ☐ No |

Does your child —	play with blocks, boxes, cups, or other construction toys without help?	☐ Yes ☐ No
	use crayons and/or markers to scribble or draw?	☐ Yes ☐ No
	listen to stories being read?	☐ Yes ☐ No
	turn pages of a book and look at pictures?	☐ Yes ☐ No
	recall stories or events?	☐ Yes ☐ No
	enjoy playing alone or with imaginary friends?	☐ Yes ☐ No
	talk with your friends/relatives who come to visit?	☐ Yes ☐ No
	follow simple, age-appropriate directions?	☐ Yes ☐ No

What are your child's favorite activities?

_____

_____

_____

Does your child have opportunites to play with other children?   ☐ Yes ☐ No

How many hours a day does your child spend watching TV? _____

| Does he or she sit very close to the TV? | ☐ Yes ☐ No |
| Does he or she turn up the volume very high? | ☐ Yes ☐ No |

Are there other things you would like to tell us about your child?

_____

_____

_____

_____

_____

_____

4

Early Childhood Curriculum, Assessment, and Program Evaluation

Building an Effective, Accountable System in Programs for Children Birth through Age 8

Adopted November 2003

A Joint Position Statement of the National Association for the Education of Young Children (NAEYC) and the National Association of Early Childhood Specialists in State Departments of Education (NAECS/SDE)

Introduction

High-quality early education produces long-lasting benefits. With this evidence, federal, state, and local decision makers are asking critical questions about young children's education. What should children be taught in the years from birth through age eight? How would we know if they are developing well and learning what we want them to learn? And how could we decide whether programs for children from infancy through the primary grades are doing a good job?

Answers to these questions—questions about *early childhood curriculum, child assessment, and program evaluation*—are the foundation of this joint position statement from the National Association for the Education of Young Children (NAEYC) and the National Association of Early Childhood Specialists in State Departments of Education (NAECS/SDE).

The Position

The National Association for the Education of Young Children and the National Association of Early Childhood Specialists in State Departments of Education take the position that policy makers, the early childhood profession, and other stakeholders in young children's lives have a shared responsibility to

- construct comprehensive systems of curriculum, assessment, and program evaluation guided by sound early childhood practices, effective early learning standards and program standards, and a set of core principles and values: belief in civic and democratic values; commitment to ethical behavior on behalf of children; use of important goals as guides to action; coordinated systems; support for children as individuals and members of families, cultures, and communities; partnerships with families; respect for evidence; and shared accountability.

- implement curriculum that is thoughtfully planned, challenging, engaging, developmentally appropriate, culturally and linguistically responsive, comprehensive, and likely to promote positive outcomes for all young children.

- make ethical, appropriate, valid, and reliable assessment a central part of all early childhood programs. To assess young children's strengths, progress, and needs, use assessment methods that are developmentally appropriate, culturally and linguistically responsive, tied to children's daily activities, supported by professional development, inclusive of families, and connected to specific, beneficial purposes: (1) making sound decisions about teaching and learning, (2) identifying significant concerns that may require focused intervention for individual children, and (3) helping programs improve their educational and developmental interventions.

- regularly engage in program evaluation guided by program goals and using varied, appropriate, conceptually and technically sound evidence to determine the extent to which programs meet the expected standards of quality and to examine intended as well as unintended results.

• provide the support, professional development, and other resources to allow staff in early childhood programs to implement high-quality curriculum, assessment, and program evaluation practices and to connect those practices with well-defined early learning standards and program standards.

Recommendations

Curriculum

Implement curriculum that is thoughtfully planned, challenging, engaging, developmentally appropriate, culturally and linguistically responsive, comprehensive, and likely to promote positive outcomes for all young children.

Indicators of Effectiveness

• *Children are active and engaged.*
Children from babyhood through primary grades—and beyond—need to be cognitively, physically, socially, and artistically active. In their own ways, children of all ages and abilities can become interested and engaged, develop positive attitudes toward learning, and have their feelings of security, emotional competence, and linkages to family and community supported.

• *Goals are clear and shared by all.*
Curriculum goals are clearly defined, shared, and understood by all "stakeholders" (for example, program administrators, teachers, and families). The curriculum and related activities and teaching strategies are designed to help achieve these goals in a unified, coherent way.

• *Curriculum is evidence-based.*
The curriculum is based on evidence that is developmentally, culturally, and linguistically relevant for the children who will experience the curriculum. It is organized around principles of child development and learning.

- *Valued content is learned through investigation, play, and focused, intentional teaching.*

Children learn by exploring, thinking about, and inquiring about all sorts of phenomena. These experiences help children investigate "big ideas," those that are important at any age and are connected to later learning. Pedagogy or teaching strategies are tailored to children's ages, developmental capacities, language and culture, and abilities or disabilities.

- *Curriculum builds on prior learning and experiences.*

The content and implementation of the curriculum builds on children's prior individual, age-related, and cultural learning, is inclusive of children with disabilities, and is supportive of background knowledge gained at home and in the community. The curriculum supports children whose home language is not English in building a solid base for later learning.

- *Curriculum is comprehensive.*

The curriculum encompasses critical areas of development including children's physical well-being and motor development; social and emotional development; approaches to learning; language development; and cognition and general knowledge; and subject matter areas such as science, mathematics, language, literacy, social studies, and the arts (more fully and explicitly for older children).

- *Professional standards validate the curriculum's subject-matter content.*

When subject-specific curricula are adopted, they meet the standards of relevant professional organizations (for example, the American Alliance for Health, Physical Education, Recreation and Dance [AAHPERD], the National Association for Music Education [MENC]; the National Council of Teachers of English [NCTE]; the National Council of Teachers of Mathematics [NCTM]; the National Dance Education Organization [NDEO]; the National Science Teachers Association [NSTA]) and are reviewed and implemented so that they fit together coherently.

• *The curriculum is likely to benefit children.*
Research and other evidence indicates that the curriculum, if implemented as intended, will likely have beneficial effects. These benefits include a wide range of outcomes. When evidence is not yet available, plans are developed to obtain this evidence.

Assessment of Young Children

Make ethical, appropriate, valid, and reliable assessment a central part of all early childhood programs. To assess young children's strengths, progress, and needs, use assessment methods that are developmentally appropriate, culturally and linguistically responsive, tied to children's daily activities, supported by professional development, inclusive of families, and connected to specific, beneficial purposes: (1) making sound decisions about teaching and learning, (2) identifying significant concerns that may require focused intervention for individual children, and (3) helping programs improve their educational and developmental interventions.

Indicators of Effectiveness

• *Ethical principles guide assessment practices.*
Ethical principles underlie all assessment practices. Young children are not denied opportunities or services, and decisions are not made about children on the basis of a single assessment.

• *Assessment instruments are used for their intended purposes.*
Assessments are used in ways consistent with the purposes for which they were designed. If the assessments will be used for additional purposes, they are validated for those purposes.

• *Assessments are appropriate for ages and other characteristics of children being assessed.*
Assessments are designed for and validated for use with children whose ages, cultures, home languages, socioeconomic status, abilities and disabilities, and other characteristics are similar to those of the children with whom the assessments will be used.

- *Assessment instruments are in compliance with professional criteria for quality.*

Assessments are valid and reliable. Accepted professional standards of quality are the basis for selection, use, and interpretation of assessment instruments, including screening tools. NAEYC and NAECS/SDE support and adhere to the measurement standards set forth in 1999 by the American Educational Research Association, the American Psychological Association, and the National Center for Measurement in Education. When individual norm-referenced tests are used, they meet these guidelines.

- *What is assessed is developmentally and educationally significant.*

The objects of assessment include a comprehensive, developmentally, and educationally important set of goals, rather than a narrow set of skills. Assessments are aligned with early learning standards, with program goals, and with specific emphases in the curriculum.

- *Assessment evidence is used to understand and improve learning.*

Assessments lead to improved knowledge about children. This knowledge is translated into improved curriculum implementation and teaching practices. Assessment helps early childhood professionals understand the learning of a specific child or group of children; enhance overall knowledge of child development; improve educational programs for young children while supporting continuity across grades and settings; and access resources and supports for children with specific needs.

- *Assessment evidence is gathered from realistic settings and situations that reflect children's actual performance.*

To influence teaching strategies or to identify children in need of further evaluation, the evidence used to assess young children's characteristics and progress is derived from real-world classroom or family contexts that are consistent with children's culture, language, and experiences.

- *Assessments use multiple sources of evidence gathered over time.*

The assessment system emphasizes repeated, systematic observation, documentation, and other forms of criterion- or performance-oriented assessment using broad, varied, and complementary methods with accommodations for children with disabilities.

• *Screening is always linked to follow-up.*
When a screening or other assessment identifies concerns, appropriate follow-up, referral, or other intervention is used. Diagnosis or labeling is never the result of a brief screening or one-time assessment.

• *Use of individually administered, norm-referenced tests is limited.*
The use of formal standardized testing and norm-referenced assessments of young children is limited to situations in which such measures are appropriate and potentially beneficial, such as identifying potential disabilities. (See also the indicator concerning the use of individual norm-referenced tests as part of program evaluation and accountability.)

• *Staff and families are knowledgeable about assessment.*
Staff are given resources that support their knowledge and skills about early childhood assessment and their ability to assess children in culturally and linguistically appropriate ways. Preservice and inservice training builds teachers' and administrators' "assessment literacy," creating a community that sees assessment as a tool to improve outcomes for children. Families are part of this community, with regular communication, partnership, and involvement.

Program Evaluation and Accountability

Regularly evaluate early childhood programs in light of program goals, using varied, appropriate, conceptually and technically sound evidence to determine the extent to which programs meet the expected standards of quality and to examine intended as well as unintended results.

Indicators of Effectiveness

• *Evaluation is used for continuous improvement.*
Programs undertake regular evaluation, including self-evaluation, to

document the extent to which they are achieving desired results, with the goal of engaging in continuous improvement. Evaluations focus on processes and implementation as well as outcomes. Over time, evidence is gathered that program evaluations do influence specific improvements.

• *Goals become guides for evaluation.*
Evaluation designs and measures are guided by goals identified by the program, by families and other stakeholders, and by the developers of a program or curriculum, while also allowing the evaluation to reveal unintended consequences.

• *Comprehensive goals are used.*
The program goals used to guide the evaluation are comprehensive, including goals related to families, teachers and other staff, and community as well as child-oriented goals that address a broad set of developmental and learning outcomes.

• *Evaluations use valid designs.*
Programs are evaluated using scientifically valid designs, guided by a "logic model" that describes ways in which the program sees its interventions having both medium- and longer-term effects on children and, in some cases, families and communities.

• *Multiple sources of data are available.*
An effective evaluation system should include multiple measures, including program data, child demographic data, information about staff qualifications, administrative practices, classroom quality assessments, implementation data, and other information that provides a context for interpreting the results of child assessments.

• *Sampling is used when assessing individual children as part of large-scale program evaluation.*
When individually administered, norm-referenced tests of children's progress are used as part of program evaluation and accountability, matrix sampling is used (that is, administered only to a systematic sample of children) so as to diminish the burden of testing on

children and to reduce the likelihood that data will be inappropriately used to make judgments about individual children.

- *Safeguards are in place if standardized tests are used as part of evaluations.*

When individually administered, norm-referenced tests are used as part of program evaluation, they must be developmentally and culturally appropriate for the particular children in the program, conducted in the language children are most comfortable with, with other accommodations as appropriate, valid in terms of the curriculum, and technically sound (including reliability and validity). Quality checks on data are conducted regularly, and the system includes multiple data sources collected over time.

- *Children's gains over time are emphasized.*

When child assessments are used as part of program evaluation, the primary focus is on children's gains or progress as documented in observations, samples of classroom work, and other assessments over the duration of the program. The focus is not just on children's scores upon exit from the program.

- *Well-trained individuals conduct evaluations.*

Program evaluations, at whatever level or scope, are conducted by well-trained individuals who are able to evaluate programs in fair and unbiased ways. Self-assessment processes used as part of comprehensive program evaluation follow a valid model. Assessor training goes beyond single workshops and includes ongoing quality checks. Data are analyzed systematically and can be quantified or aggregated to provide evidence of the extent to which the program is meeting its goals.

- *Evaluation results are publicly shared.*

Families, policy makers, and other stakeholders have the right to know the results of program evaluations. Data from program monitoring and evaluation, aggregated appropriately and based on reliable measures, should be made available and accessible to the public.

Creating Change through Support for Programs

Implementing the preceding recommendations for curriculum, child assessment, and program evaluation requires a solid foundation. Calls for better results and greater accountability from programs for children in preschool, kindergarten, and the primary grades have not been backed up by essential supports for teacher recruitment and compensation, professional preparation and ongoing professional development, and other ingredients of quality early education.

The overarching need is to create an integrated, well-financed system of early care and education that has the capacity to support learning and development in all children, including children living in poverty, children whose home language is not English, and children with disabilities. Unlike many other countries, the United States continues to have a fragmented system for educating children from birth through age eight, under multiple auspices, with greatly varying levels of support, and with inadequate communication and collaboration.

Many challenges face efforts to provide all young children with high-quality curriculum, assessment, and evaluation of their programs. Public commitment, along with investments in a well-financed system of early childhood education and in other components of services for young children and their families, will make it possible to implement these recommendations fully and effectively.

Early years are learning years

Become a member of NAEYC, and help make them count!

Just as you help young children learn and grow, the National Association for the Education of Young Children—your professional organization—supports you in the work you love. NAEYC is the world's largest early childhood education organization, with a national network of local, state, and regional Affiliates. We are more than 100,000 members working together to bring high-quality early learning opportunities to all children from birth through age eight.

Since 1926, NAEYC has provided educational services and resources for people working with children, including:

• *Young Children*, the award-winning journal (six issues a year) for early childhood educators

• **Books, posters, brochures, and videos** to support your work with young children and families

• **The NAEYC Annual Conference**, which brings tens of thousands of people together from across the country and around the world to share their expertise and ideas on the education of young children

• **Insurance plans** for members and programs

• **A voluntary accreditation system** to help programs reach national standards for high-quality early childhood education

• **Young Children International** to promote global communication and information exchanges

• **www.naeyc.org**—a dynamic Website with up-to-date information on all of our services and resources

To join NAEYC

To find a complete list of membership benefits and options or to join NAEYC online, visit **www.naeyc.org/membership.** Or you can mail this form to us.

(Membership must be for an individual, not a center or school.)

Name _____

Address_____

City_____ State_____ ZIP_____

E-mail _____

Phone (H)_____ (W)_____

❏ New member

❏ Renewal ID # _____

Affiliate name/number _____

To determine your dues, you must visit **www.naeyc.org/membership** or call 800-424-2460, ext. 2002.

Indicate your payment option

❏ VISA   ❏ MasterCard

Card # _____

Exp. date _____

Cardholder's name _____

Signature _____

Note: By joining NAEYC you also become a member of your state and local Affiliates.

Send this form and payment to

NAEYC
PO Box 97156
Washington, DC 20090-7156